JORDAN

JORDAN'S HISTORY AT A GLANCE

8500-4500 BC	Neolithic Period
4500-3300 BC	Chalcolithic Period
3300-1200 BC	Bronze Age
1200-539 BC	Iron Age
539-332 BC	Babylonian and Persian Periods
Fourth Century BC-106 BC	Nabatean Kingdom
332-63 BC	Hellenistic Period
63 BC-324 AD	Roman Empire
324-640	Byzantine Period
640-1291	Islamic Middle Ages
661-750	Umayyad Caliphs
750-969	Abbasid Caliphs
969-1171	Fatimid Caliphs
1171-1263	Ayyubid Caliphs
1099-1291	Crusaders
1250-1517	Mamluk Caliphs
1517-1918	Ottoman Empire
1916-1918	Arab Revolt
1921	Emirate of Transjordan established
1946	Transjordan gains independence
1950	New Name: Hashemite Kingdom of Jordan

All rights reserved. No part of this publication may be reproduced in any
form or by means without the prior permission of the copyright owner.
© Copyright reserved
Published by Palphot Ltd.
www.palphot.com
Text: Carl Schrag
Photography: Garo Nalbandian
Photo on page 3 by Zohrab Markarian
ISBN 965-280-080-5
Printed in Israel

His Late Majesty King Hussein
of the Hashemite Kingdom of Jordan
——— 1935 - 1999 ———

Contents

GOLAN HEIGHTS

SYRIA

Haifa

SEA OF GALILEE

Tiberias

Nazareth

River Yarmouk

Umm Qeis (Gadera)

JEBEL EL-DRUZE

Pella

GILEAD

Ajlun

Umm el-Jimal

Jerash

WADI ZARQA (JABOK)

Qasr el-Hallabat

River Jordan

JORDAN VALLEY

ZARQA

Tel Aviv

AMMAN

AMMON

Azraq

ISRAEL

Qasr Amra

AZRAQ OASIS

Jericho

Qasr Mushatta

MOUNT NEBO

Qasr Kharana

JERUSALEM

Madaba

Bethlehem

DEAD SEA

Mukawir (Machaerus)

WADI MUJIB (ARNON)

Qasr el-Tuba

MOAB

Masada

JORDAN

Kerak Castle

Beer Sheba

WADI HASA (ZERED)

Dana

Shobak Castle

WADI ARABAH

Petra

WADI MOUSA

EDOM

SAUDI ARABIA

EGYPT

Eilat

Aqaba

Tabah

WADI RUM

GULF OF AQABA

INTRODUCTION

The Hashemite Kingdom of Jordan combines ancient history and modernity in a fascinating old-new land. Landlocked, except for a tiny outlet to the Red Sea at Aqaba, this desert has blossomed in recent decades into a modern country that meshes ancient delights and Middle Eastern hospitality with a high level of education, advanced communications systems and a fascinating capital city that encapsulates the past and future of Jordan.

Nearly lost to Western visitors until the early nineteenth century, Jordan has been a cradle of civilization since time immemorial. Man has lived in what is today Jordan for more than a million years. While little remains of those earliest residents, the country is filled with archeological sites attesting to other periods of ancient settlement.

As long ago as 3200 BC, Jordan was a particularly urban region. But the country is best-known today for the remarkable stone-cut architecture of the Nabateans in Petra. During the Hellenistic period, they made this city their capital.

For many hundreds of years, Petra - and, indeed, most of Jordan - was beyond the realm of Western travellers. Then, in the nineteenth century, a few determined, intrepid travellers penetrated the centuries of isolation. They brought tales of a fascinating desert land to the West, and Petra, Jerash, Madaba, the Desert Castles and the country's other attractions became increasingly popular tourist destinations.

Today, Jordan puts out the welcome mat for visitors from all over the world. The descendants of the locals who used to chase away outsiders have learned to be among the world's warmest hosts.

Left: Jerash, one of the world's best-preserved Roman cities
Below: A Beduin rides his "desert horse"
Overleaf: Bird's eye view of Amman

MOSQUES OF AMMAN - At the heart of downtown Amman, the Al-Husseini Mosque was built in Ottoman style in 1924 on the site of an ancient mosque and the cathedral of Philadelphia. The Darwish Mosque (below) was built in 1961 on a hill overlooking the city by a Circassian.

Above: *The city centre*

AMMAN

The capital of the Hashemite Kingdom of Jordan since the country gained independence in 1946, Amman is an ultra-modern metropolis that boasts a history of nearly continuous inhabitation over the past 9,000 years. Recently, it has grown dramatically. Its residential and business districts extend over an ever-growing number of hills that are connected by a sophisticated and efficient road network, and its population numbers 1.5 million people.

Amman is Jordan's business and administrative centre. By day, its open-air markets bustle with people buying everything from carrots and figs to living room furniture in stalls and shops that line the streets and alleyways. Countless grill restaurants beckon, offering local delicacies such as kabob, felafel, hoummus and assorted other meats and salads.

When the muezzin calls the faithful to prayer, people head straight for the many mosques that dot the city's landscape. Some of them, like the al-Husseini Mosque in the centre of the city, are magnificent works of architecture.

Others can be as simple as a small room off of a side street. At night, the city centre takes on a spicy flavour, and fashionable cafes along the broad avenues of the Shmeisani district are filled with young and old Jordanians and visitors who watch the people stroll by as they sip coffee and smoke fruit-flavoured tobacco in tall standing pipes. Amman was not always as large and bustling as it is today. First mentioned in the Bible in Deuteronomy 3, as Rabbat-Ammon, the capital of the Ammonites, the prophets Jeremiah and Ezekiel each predicted that Nebuchadnezzar would conquer the city, but they were proved wrong; the Babylonian ruler took Jerusalem instead.

In the Hellenistic Period (about 300-65 BC), the city was ruled by the Syrian Seleucids and the Egyptian Ptolemies, who conquered it from each other several times. In the third century BC, it was renamed Philadelphia by Ptolemy II Philadelphus, who conquered the city and wanted to associate it with his own name. Later, the Nabateans held it briefly, but Herod took it from them.

Philadelphia was one of the ten cities of the Roman Decapolis, and the Romans built it rapidly and ambitiously. The most impressive remnant of their rule is the well-preserved theatre at the heart of the city.

Philadelphia prospered throughout the Roman, Byzantine and Arab periods, but it then began to decline. By the fifteenth century, it was empty and in veritable ruins. Through 400 years of Ottoman Turkish rule, the place remained neglected, although the Sultan did send a small community of Circassians to settle among the ruins in 1878.

Only in 1921, when Emir Abdullah of the prestigious Beduin Hashemite family took the reins of the new entity of Transjordan and chose Amman as his capital did the city begin to thrive again. It grew steadily, and after Jordan gained independence in 1946 its population was bolstered by successive influxes of newcomers.

Today, the historic area of Philadelphia lies at the heart of a sprawling, aesthetically pleasing mixture of private homes, apartment complexes, office buildings, public facilities, parks and open spaces.

THE ROMAN THEATRE

Built into the side of a mountain in the late second century AD by Antoninus Pius, the theatre has room for 6,000 people. Restoration began in 1960, and the theatre today is a prime example of Roman architecture. Adjacent are the remains of the Odeon, or covered hall, which was built in the third century AD.

CITADEL HILL

High atop the Roman Theatre and the rest of downtown Amman, this plateau is the site of the ancient city of Rabbat - Ammon. Amid the Byzantine and Umayyad ruins, the main attractions are the panoramic view of the sprawling city and the surrounding desert plains, and the Amman Archeological Museum, which is nestled behind the remains of a second century Roman temple.

Below: *The Roman Theatre in Amman*
Right: *Panoramic view of Amman from above the Roman Theatre*

CAVE OF THE SEVEN SLEEPERS

Adjacent to the Ahl el-Kahf Mosque is the Cave of the Seven Sleepers, the subject of a legend subscribed to both by Christians and Moslems. The story tells of six Christian boys who lived near Philadelphia during the reign of a pagan ruler who threatened to kill them. They fled and, together with a shepherd and his dog, hid in a cave, where they slept for anywhere between 30 and 309 years. Upon waking, they went to Philadelphia and tried to use their Roman coins to buy food. When the population realized what had happened, the boys were honoured by Theodosius, who ruled the city. Afterwards, they returned to the cave and God sent them back to sleep.

Today, eight small tombs stand in the Cave of the Seven Sleepers. One has been opened, and visitors can see what appears to be seven skulls and the remains of a dog.

SWEIFIEH MOSAIC

At the western end of town, this impressive Byzantine mosaic was discovered by construction crews, and it was restored in 1970 by a joint Jordanian-American team. Dating from the sixth century, the mosaic adorned the floor of a Byzantine church, and its high-quality depictions of people and animals indicate that it was created by master craftsmen. Immediately beneath it is another, older mosaic floor that has not been excavated.

Below: The ruins of Philadelphia on the Citadel
Top Right: The Cave of the Seven Sleepers
Bottom Right: The remains of a sixth century Byzantine church on the Citadel

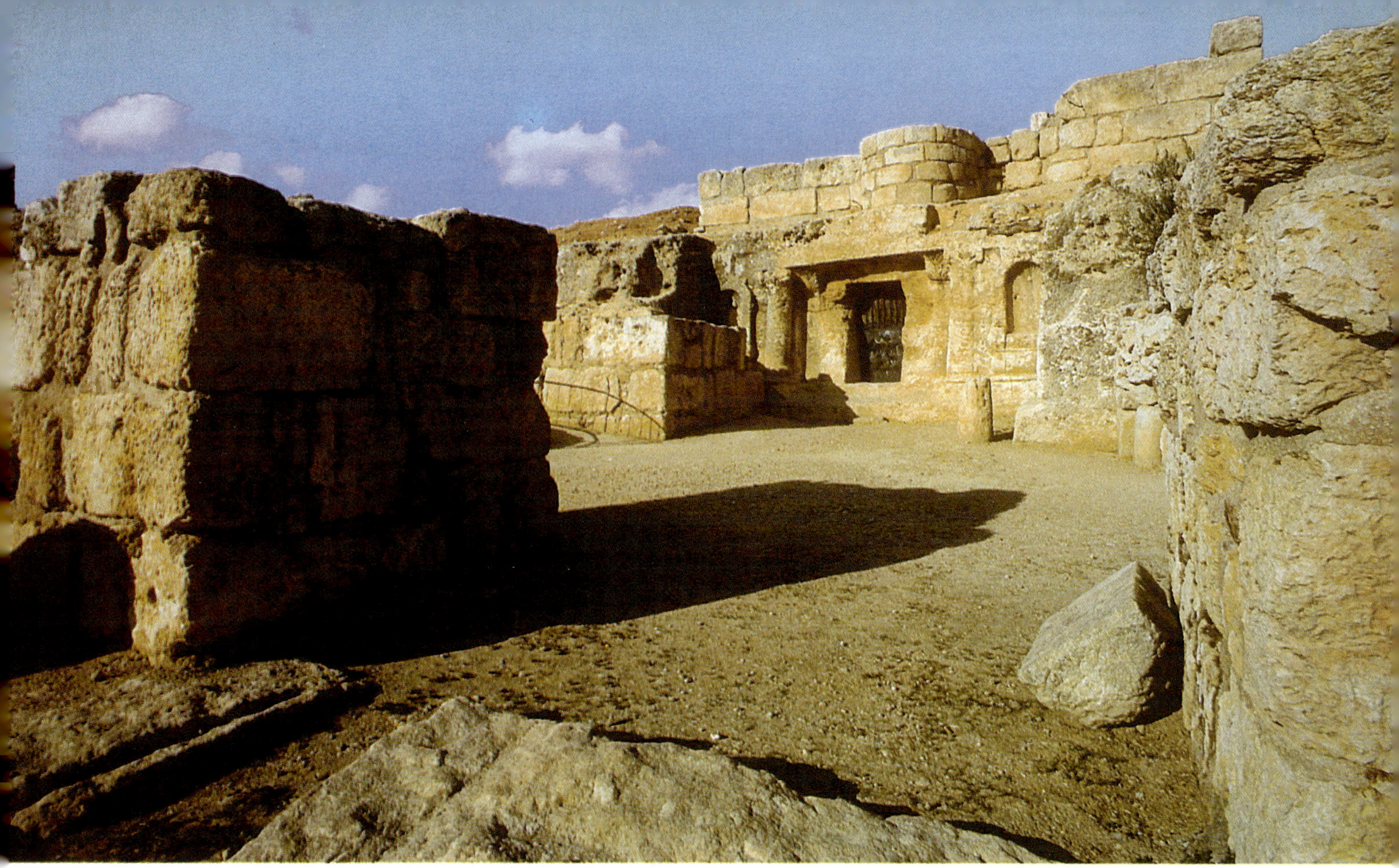

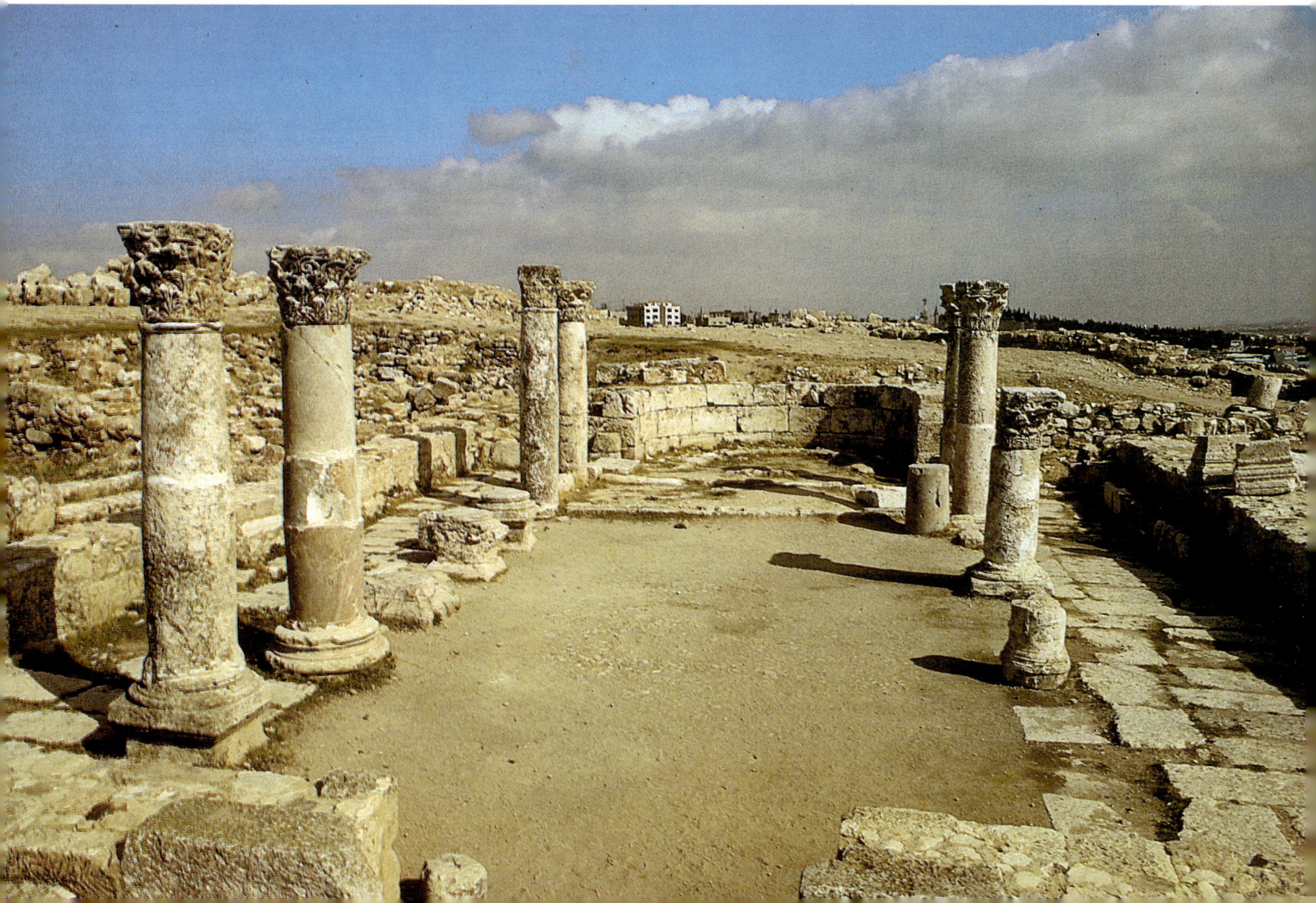

Above: *The Amman Archeological Museum*
Left and Right: *From the museum's exhibition, sculpture tells the story of Jordan's ancient history*
near left, top: *from the Temple of the Winged Lions, Petra;*
near left, bottom: *double-faced female head, from the Amman Citadel; bottom right, Head of Tyche (Fortune), dating from the second century AD)*

THEATRE MUSEUMS

Two fine museums occupy the wings of the Roman Theatre. The Jordan Museum of Folklore and the Museum of Costumes and Jewelry display a collection of mosaics from Madaba, Jerash and elsewhere, as well as mannequins dressed in traditional garb. The intricacies of regional embroidery are explained, and fine specimens of Beduin and Palestinian crafts are on display.

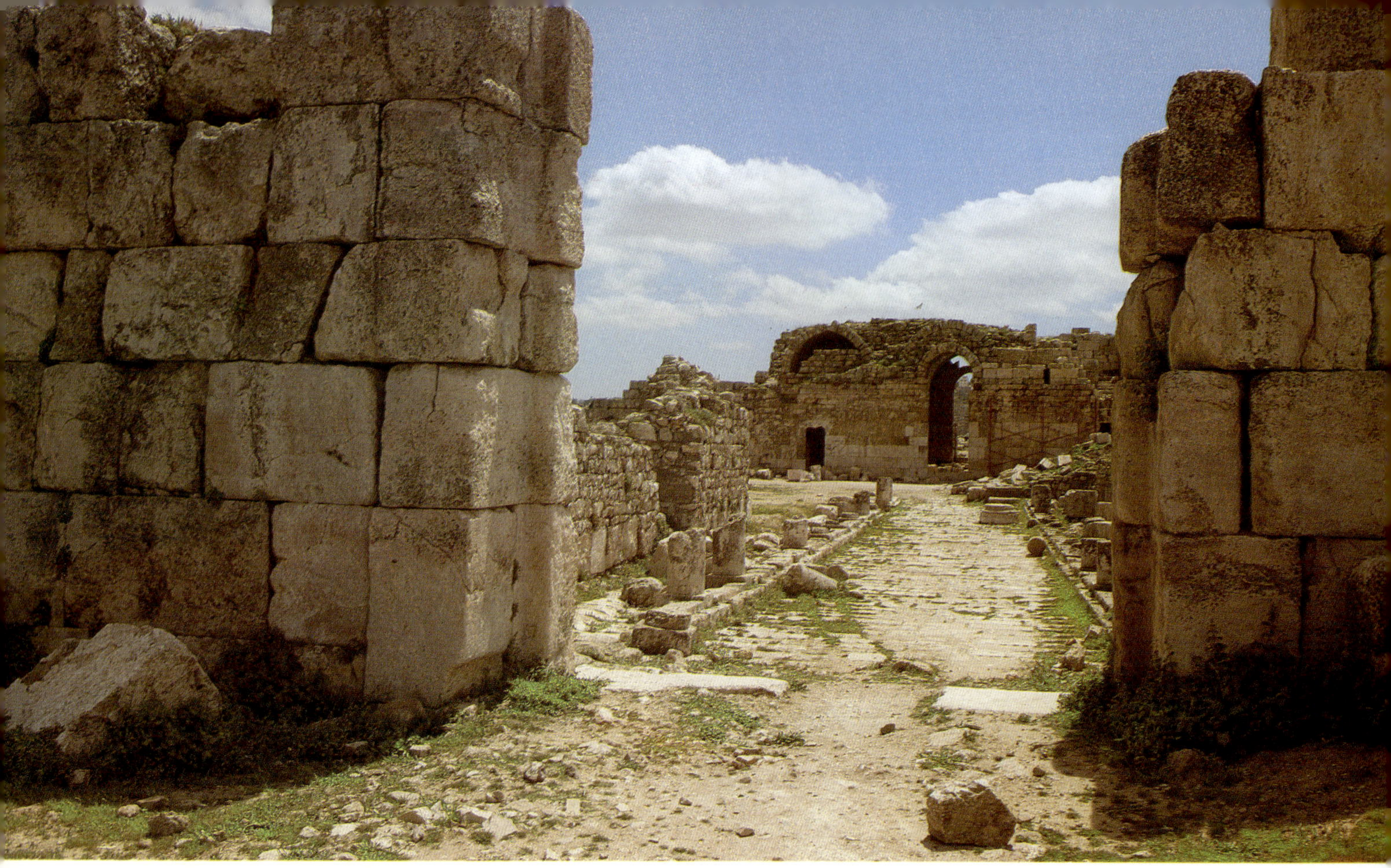

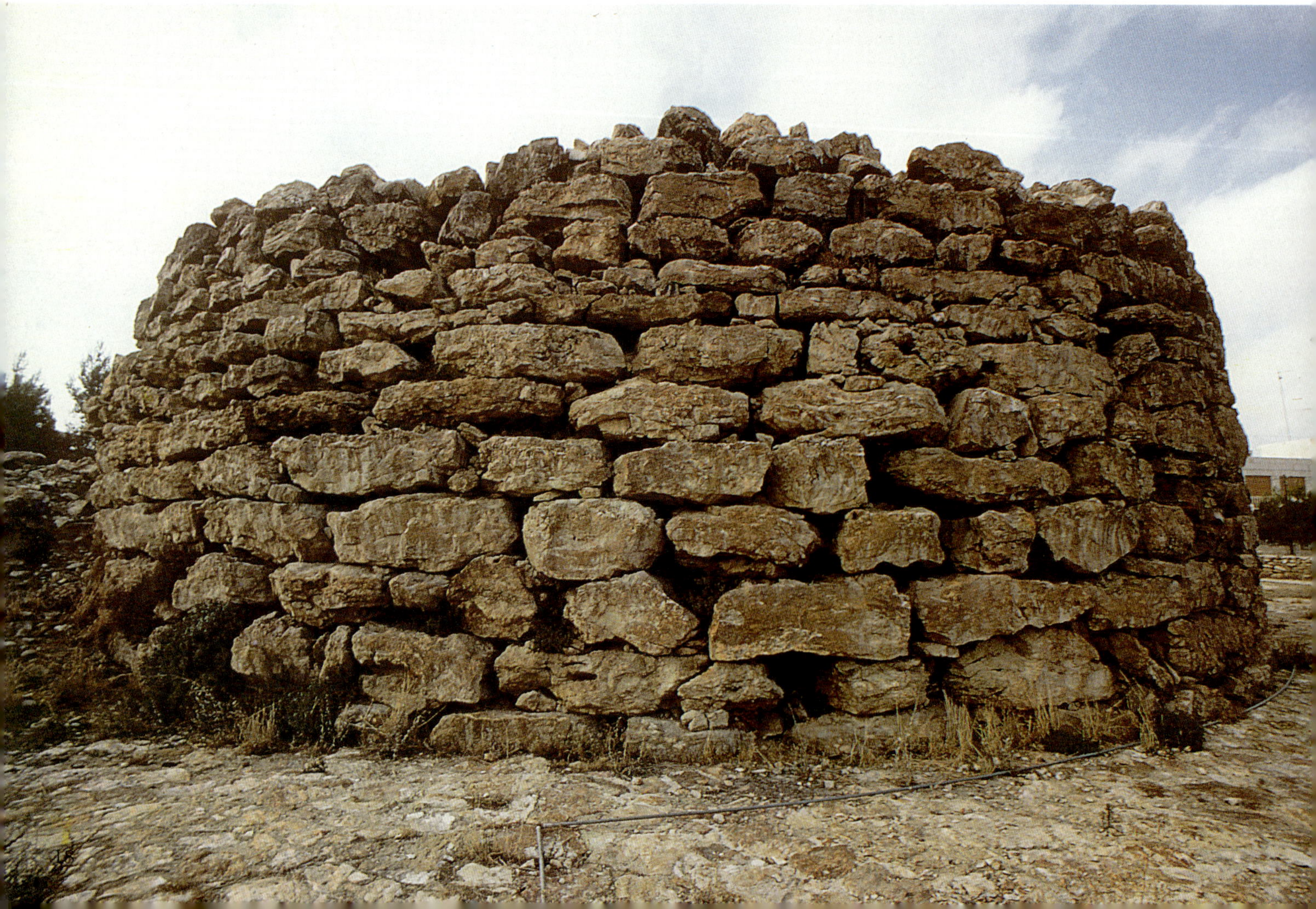

AMMONITE TOWERS

For years, the remains of more than two dozen towers built of huge stones have puzzled archeologists. Located in and around Amman, the towers were recently dated to the late Iron Age (specifically, the seventh and sixth centuries B.C.) Many of them have been destroyed in the path of development, but two prime specimens remain, at Malfouf and Khirbet Sar.

Far Left, Top: *Islamic ruins on the Citadel*
Far Left, Bottom: *Ammonite tower at Malfouf*
Left and Below: *Roman ruins in Amman*

IRAQ EL AMIR

Twenty kilometres west of Amman lie the remains of the best-preserved Hellenistic site in the country, Iraq el-Amir. It served as the estate of the Tobiad family, whose name is inscribed on the wall. Called Qasr el-Abd (The Castle of the Slave), it was built around 187-175 BC, and it is a two storey rectangular building, with each storey divided into a series of rooms and passageways. Many of the huge stone blocks used to build the structure featurs sculpted lions and eagles.

Left, Above and Below: *Iraq el-Amir*

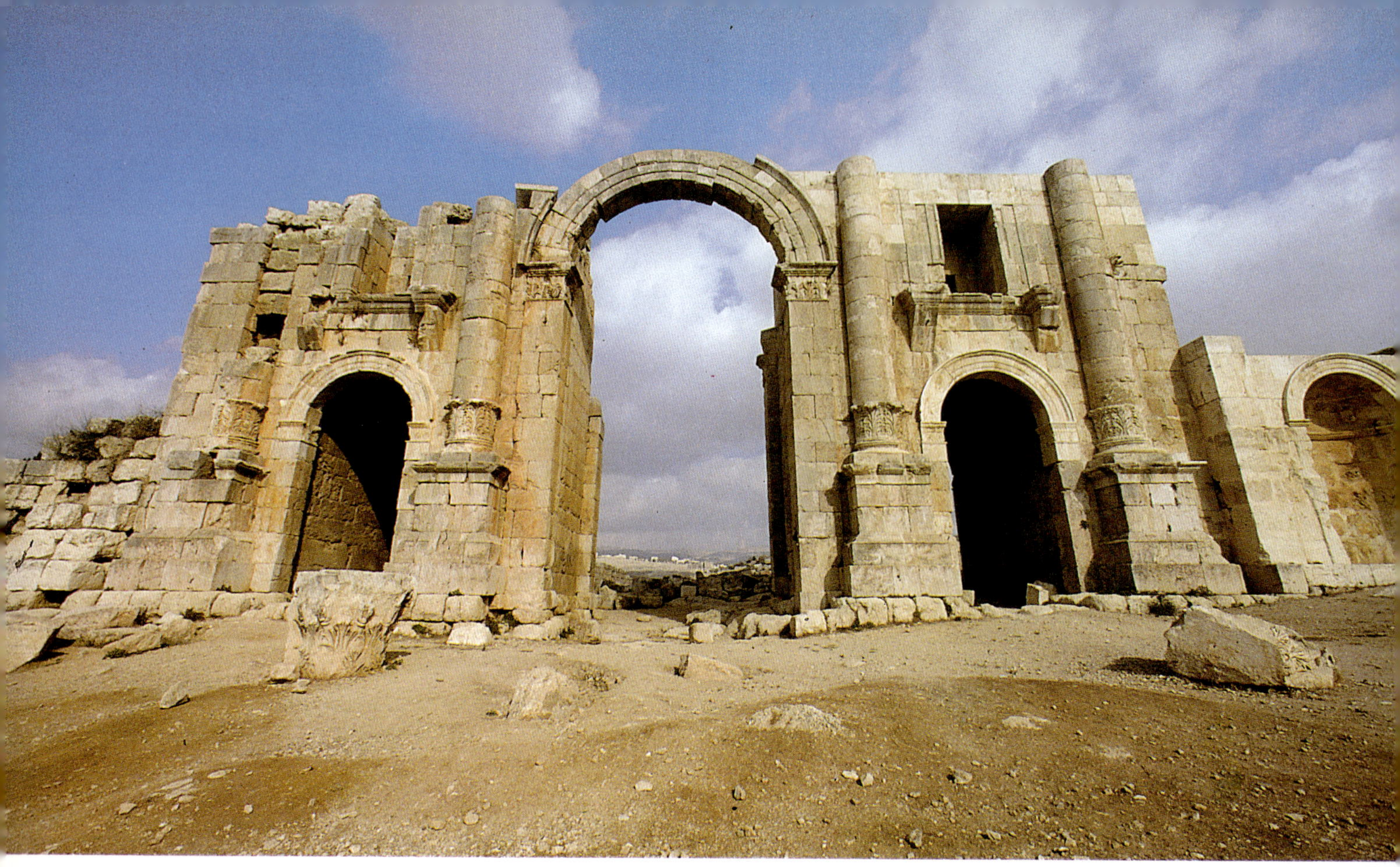

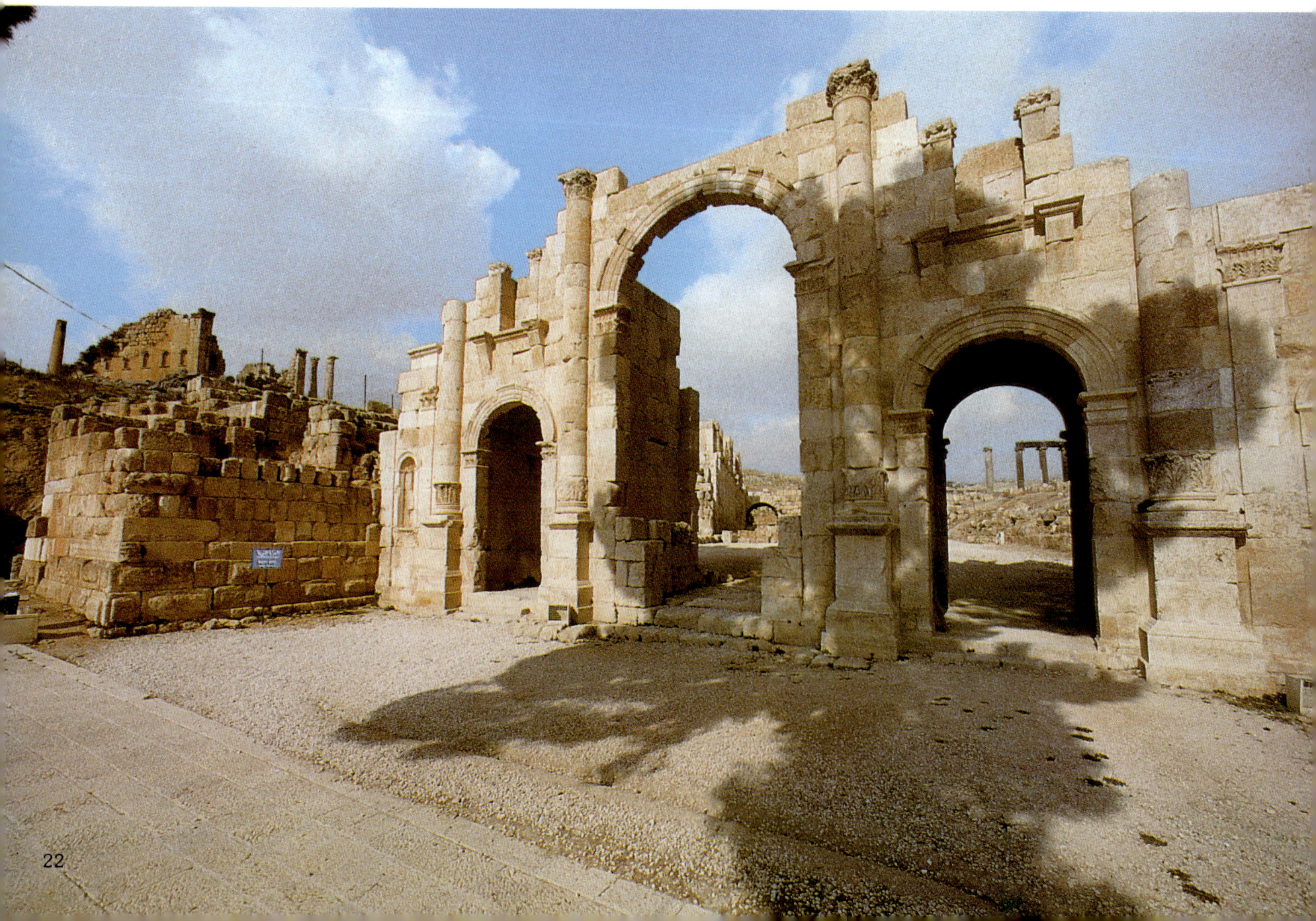

JERASH

Less than 50 kilometres north of Amman, nestled in the Gilead mountains, lies one of the best-preserved Roman provincial cities of the Decapolis, and indeed of the world. The area was populated at least since Neolithic times, or 6000 BC, but the leap from a small settlement to an important city was probably made under the rule of one of the Seleucid kings. Research points to King Antiochus IV, who ruled between 175-163 BC, as most likely responsible for transforming the place into a prominent centre.

Jerash became an important crossroads, a meeting place for East and West. Here, the Roman Empire encountered the Near East. Aside from its crucial role in trade, Jerash became the model of a new kind of Roman city built with a distinctly Oriental flavour.

Opposite Page:
Top: *Hadrian's Arch*
Bottom: *South Gate*

Right: *Zeus Temple Complex*
Below: *South Theatre*

But Jerash offers visitors much more than the ruins of an impressive Roman city. Within the complex are remains of 2,500 years of settlement, from the Bronze and Iron ages and the Hellenistic, Roman, Byzantine, Umayyad and Abbasid periods, spanning from about 1600 BC through 900 AD. Most of the structures are from the first through ninth centuries AD, but the museum houses a collection that includes more ancient artifacts.

In the Hellenistic period, Jerash was known as Antioch on the Chrysorhoas, or "Golden River." The little stream was no larger in those days than it is today, making the name something of a misnomer, but it has always provided a source of fresh water and made the region particularly fertile.

Like so many other sites in Jordan, Jerash was lost to the world for hundreds of years. In 1806, German researcher Ulrich Jasper Seetzen "rediscovered" the city, and it has been a popular tourist destination and the site of important archeological work ever since.

The Romans drew up a grand city plan for the place they called Gerasa around 50 or 60 AD. It was designed around a main north-south axis road, or Cardo Maximus,

Previous Page: *The Oval Plaza*
Below: *North Tetrapylon, where the Cardo met the North Decumanus*

two east-west intersecting streets with a wall protecting the whole area. Over the next two centuries, the city developed rapidly and prospered. In the third century, it was elevated to the status of a colony, but it began to decline soon thereafter.

HADRIAN'S ARCH

Approaching from the south, the first thing a visitor sees is Hadrian's Arch. A typical Roman triumphal arch, it was built to mark the visit of Emperor Hadrian in 130 A.D. The designers were a bit too optimistic about Jerash's expansion; the arch lies more than 400 metres south of the city's walls, and it never became part of the city.

Just north of the arch is Jerash's South Gate. The two, which bear similar columns and floral carvings, are connected by a perfectly straight Roman road.

THE FORUM (AGORA)

Reached through the Cardo, the Forum is a large public

Opposite Page: *Roman Meat Market*

26

building that seems to have been the main meeting place in the second century AD. The beautiful mosaic floors of the shops that lined the Forum's entryway have been reburied to preserve them.

HIPPODROME

Measuring 245 metres by 51 metres, this facility could hold 15,000 people, making it by far the largest sports and entertainment site in Jerash. Scholars have not been able to pinpoint its construction date; indeed, they are unsure whether it was ever completed and used.
Located beyond Hadrian's Arch but outside the city walls, the Hippodrome is surrounded by a Roman-Byzantine cemetery that has many rock-cut tombs where the city's wealthy residents were buried.

CITY WALLS

Continually rebuilt and expanded with Jerash's growing fortunes, the city walls were first constructed around 60 AD. What remains today is a total of 3.5 kilometres of three-metre thick walls surrounding an area of almost one square kilometre. The stream flows through the walled city.

SOUTH GATE AND SOUTH STREET

The main entry to Jerash for travellers coming from Philadelphia (Amman), this gate is very similar to Hadrian's Arch a few hundred metres further south. The South Street leads from the South Gate through an area that was populated in the second century BC, when Jerash was the site of a Hellenistic city.

NYMPHAEUM

Dating from the late second century, this fountain dedicated to the nymphs is one of the finest examples of stonecutting work from the Roman era. The red granite basin was added later, during the Byzantine period.

Opposite Page: The Cardo
Above and Left: Scenes from Roman Temples

OVAL PLAZA

The unusual shape of this plaza is probably explained by the Roman town planners' insistence on symmetry. If not for the 90 metre by 80 metre shape, the axes of the South Street and the Cardo would not have crossed properly. The column that stands at the centre of the plaza is not ancient; the Jordanians built it recently to hold the torch of the annual Jerash Festival, an international arts and culture event held each summer in the Roman theatres.

THEATRES

Jerash boasts three Roman theatres, the largest of which is the South Theatre, which could seat 3,000. Visitors can still see the Greek numbers on the seats, indicating that people could reserve seats in advance. The acoustics are exceptional, and the reconstructed stage - which features decorations carved from stone - is as ideal a setting for performances at the modern-day Jerash Festival as it was 2,000 years ago.

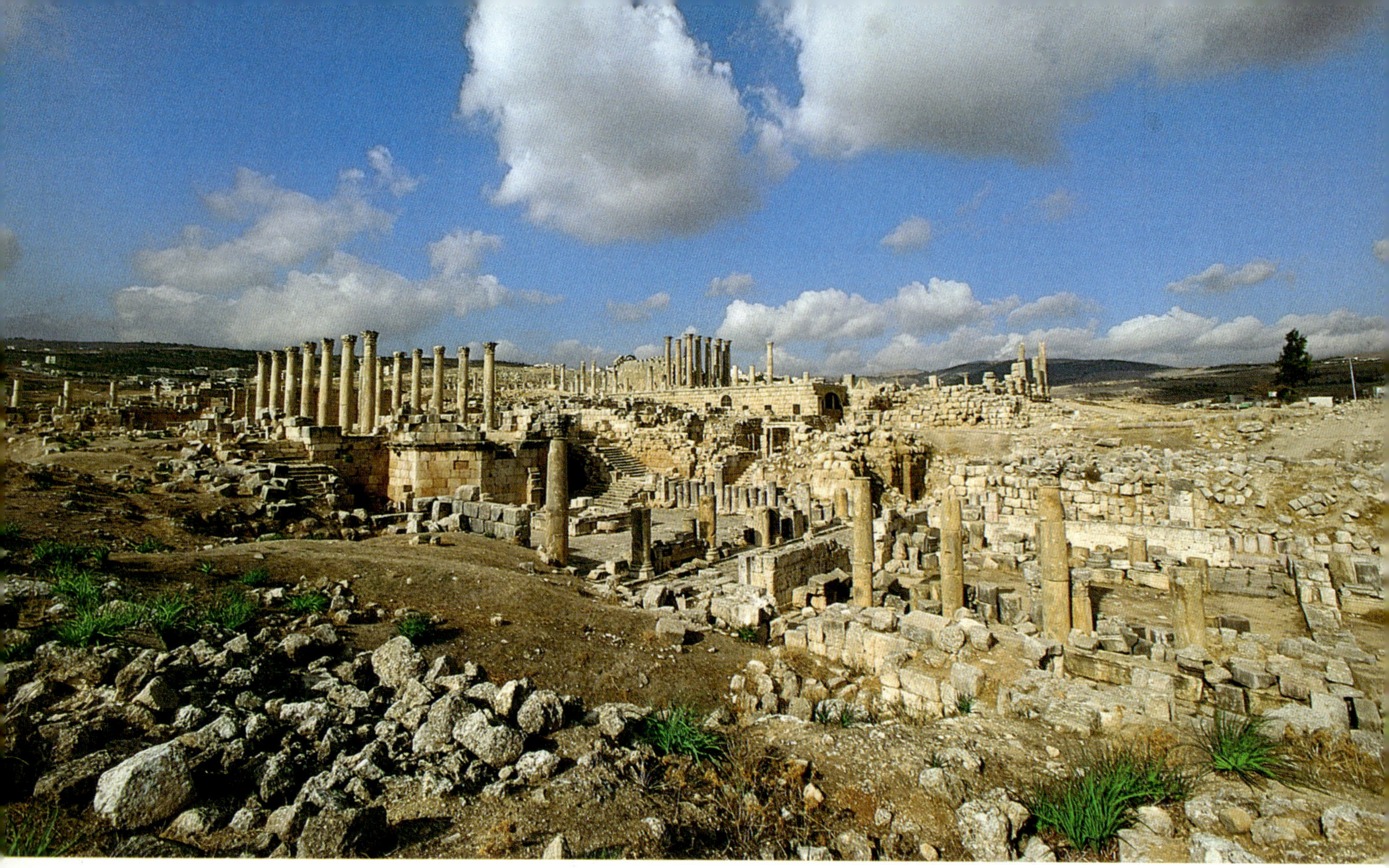

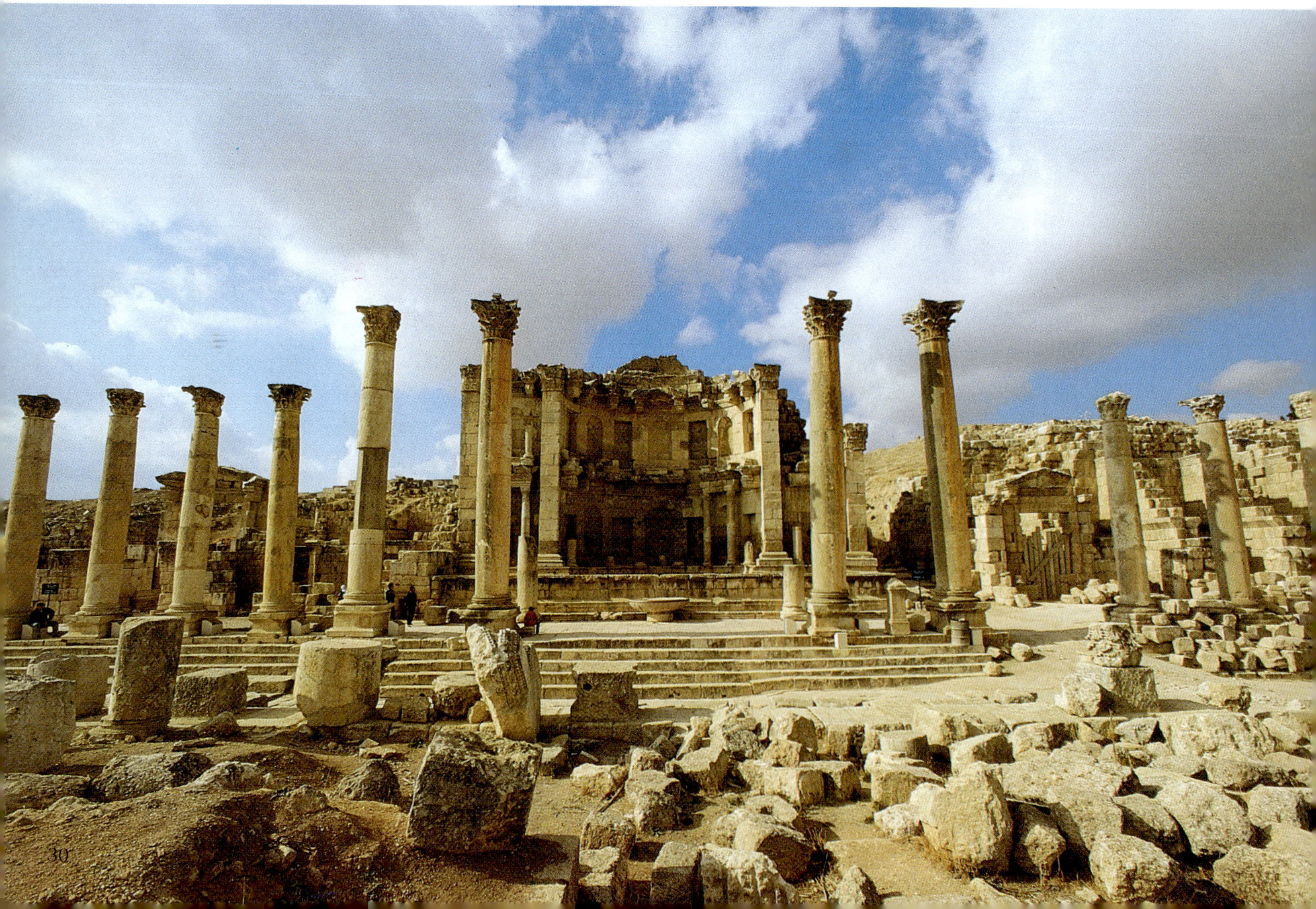

The North Theatre, which has also undergone extensive excavation, was completed in 165 AD. Originally a small covered odeon with 14 rows of seats that was used for poetry readings, plays and meetings of the city council, it underwent frequent remodelling and modification. By the time it ceased to be used, in the sixth century, it had been expanded to seat 1,600 people. It seems that a major earthquake in the mid-sixth century destroyed the theatre, and its stones were used to build many other buildings.

The Festival Theatre lies 1,500 metres north of the city's North Gate and overlooks the Birketein ("Two Pools") Reservoir. The theatre, which seats 1,000, seems to have been used for religious festivals, some of which may have included risque performances by naked women.

ZEUS TEMPLE

In all likelihood, the hilltop Zeus Temple was built in the first or second century BC, but no archeological remains that verify the date have been unearthed. Inscriptions detailing donations by wealthy town residents tell us that the first Roman sanctuary was built in the first half of the first century AD. The temple is surrounded by three

Opposite Page:
Top: *General view, with Temple of Artemis in centre background*
Bottom: *Nymphaeum*

Right: *Temple of Artemis*
Below: *Roman street view*

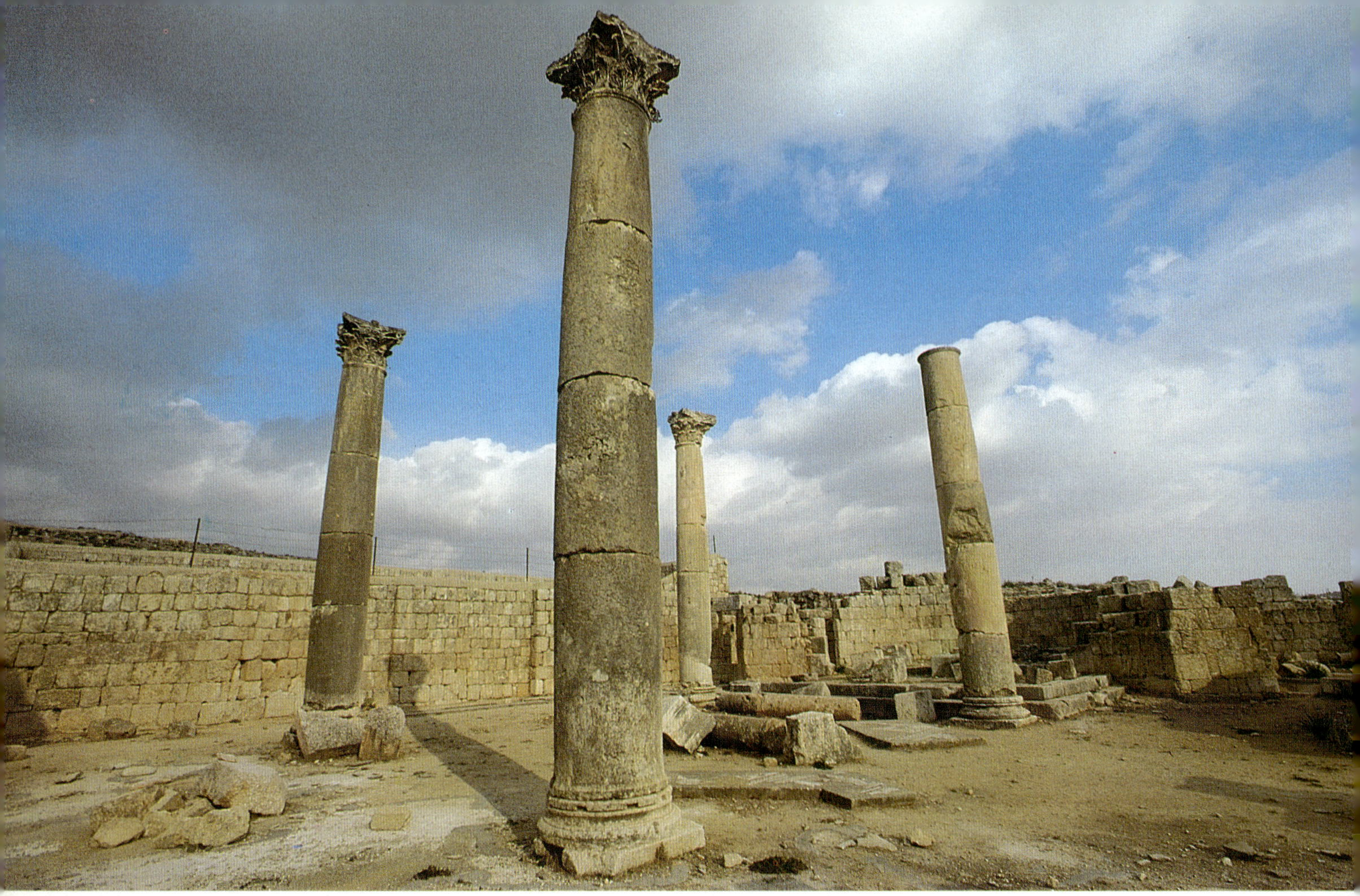

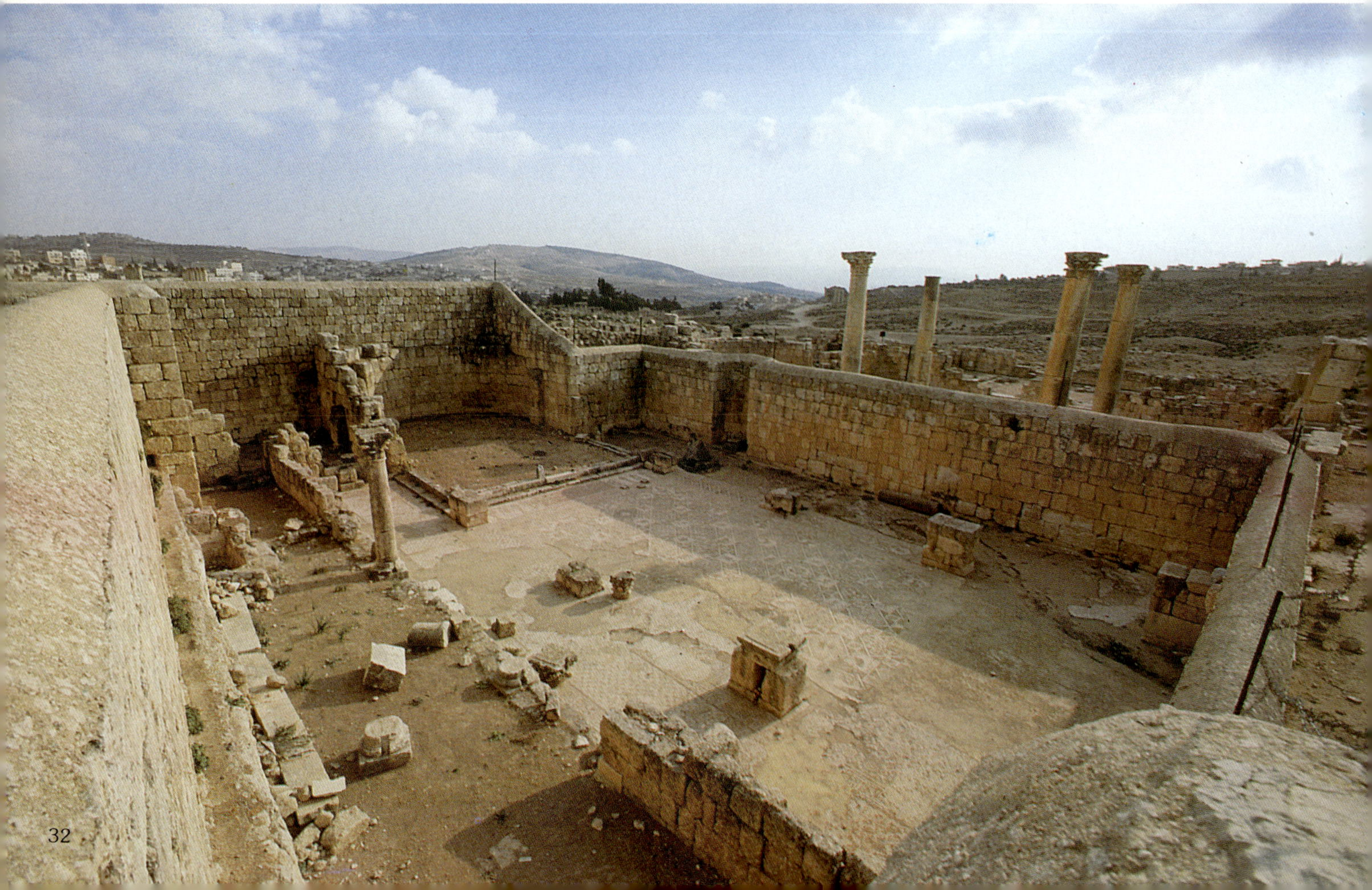

terraces called temenos, or the holy precinct. Such temenos usually encircled ancient temples in the region.

BYZANTINE CHURCHES

More than a dozen Byzantine churches have been excavated at Jerash, and others certainly remain to be "discovered." Most were built during the fifth and sixth centuries AD, and used materials taken from old Hellenistic and Roman structures. Many of the beautiful mosaic floors have been reburied to protect them, but some are on display here and in Amman.

Among the most interesting of the Byzantine churches:

CHURCH OF BISHOP ISAIAH

Built by the ruler whose name it bears, this church was completed in 559 AD, and was used until the 747

earthquake which levelled much of Jerash. Built in typical Byzantine style, the church has a central nave, two flanking aisles and mosaic floors that featured geometric, floral and faunal patterns, as well as portraits. Most of the human and animal figures in the mosaics, which have been reburied since their discovery, were defaced in the eighth and ninth centuries.

BISHOP GENESIUS CHURCH

A floor mosaic dated 611 gives this church the distinction of being the last church built in Gerasa before the arrival of the Persians in 614.

Opposite Page and Below: *Views of the columns and mosaic floor of the Church of SS Cosmas and Damian*
Next Page:
Top: *The Synagogue Church*
Bottom: *Temple of Artemis*
Page 35: *Temple of Artemis*

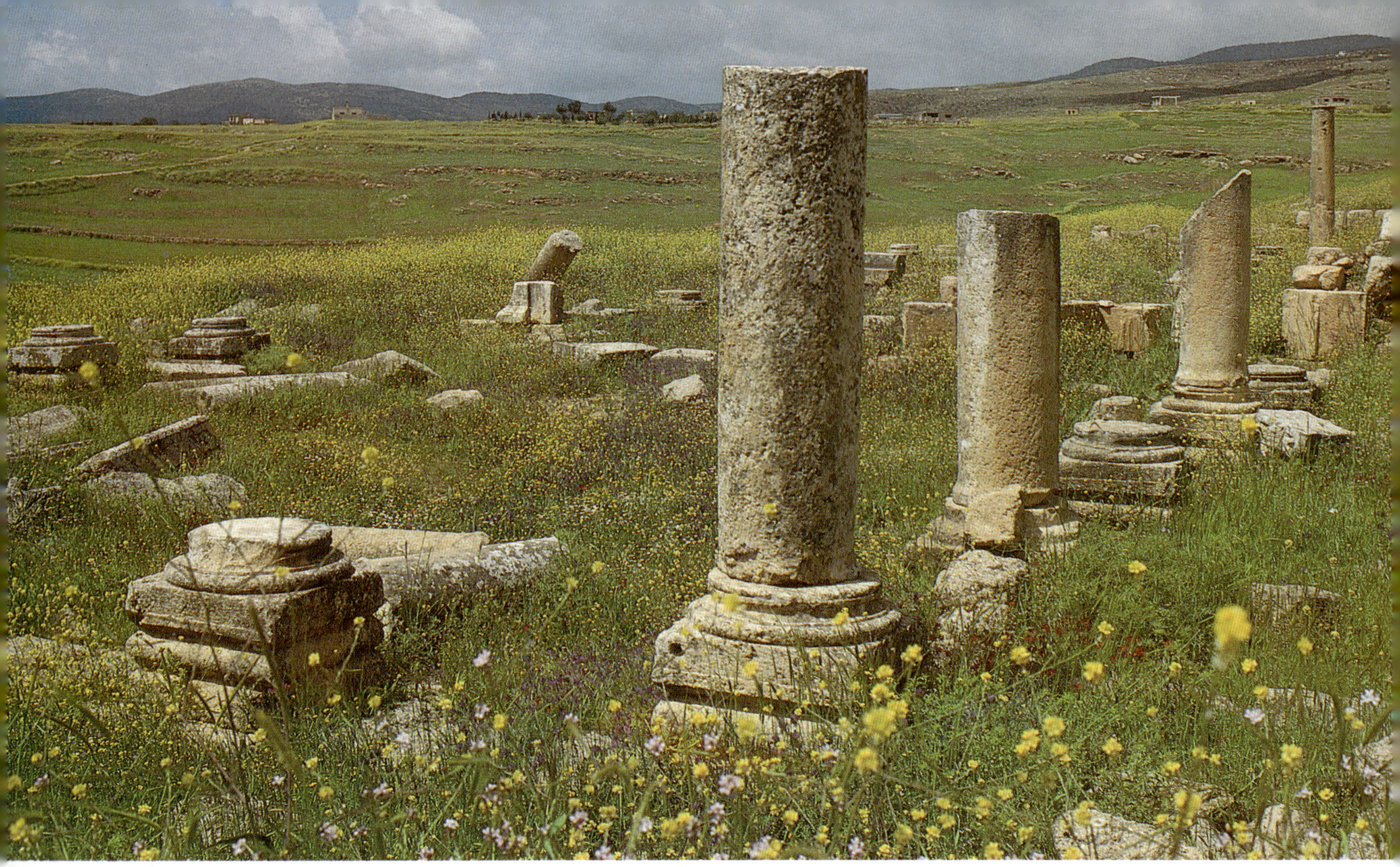

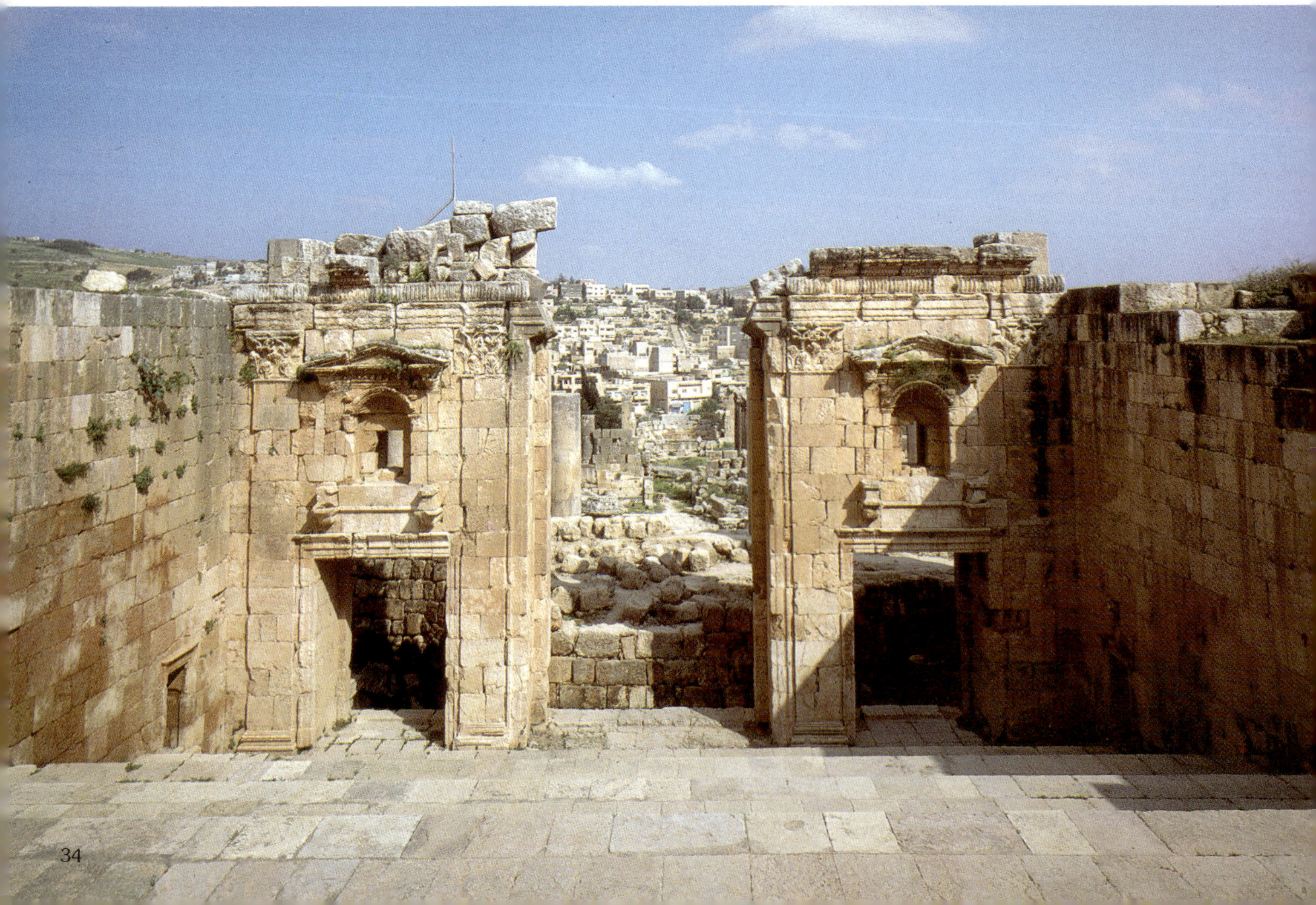

TEMPLE OF ARTEMIS

Named for the Roman goddess, the Temple of Artemis dominates Jerash. Built in the second century AD, at the height of Gerasa's prosperity, everything about the temple was lavish and extravagant - from the 100-metre staircase leading up from the Cardo to the sanctuary itself. Some scholars believe the temple was never completed. Its ruins provided the Byzantines and Umayyads with raw materials for pottery-making.

SYNAGOGUE CHURCH

This church stands on the site of a third or fourth century synagogue that was built to face west to Jerusalem. When the church was constructed in 531, the original mosaic floor - which depicted the story of Noah and the Ark - was covered with a new one.

THE CARDO

Ancient Jerash's main thoroughfare, the Cardo, extends 800 metres north from the edge of the Oval Plaza. Its Corinthian columns date from the second century AD. At the far north extreme, the Cardo is narrower and is bordered by the Ionic colonnade that was built along the entire length in the first century AD. The Cardo, which was the focal point of the ancient city, was in itself a miracle of engineering, with an advanced sewer system running beneath its entire length. The road's large stones bear evidence of the Roman chariots that rode along it every day.

THE UMAYYAD PRESENCE

Excavated and restored during the 1980s, the Umayyad housing complex was home to early Islamic Umayyads from about 660 AD. Apparently, after severe earthquake damage made the building unsuited for living quarters, it was used as the site for a pottery kiln. One Umayyad mosque, dating from the seventh or eighth century AD, has been unearthed in Jerash, a few metres from the Cardo. It made excellent use of the Roman and Byzantine remains; the mosque is housed in what had been a Roman house, and an old decorative niche was used for prayer.

Opposite Page and Below: *Temple of Artemis*

Above: *The Zarqa River (Jabok)*

The Arab castle at Aljun

WADI ZARQA (JABOK)

Passing near Jerash, and feeding into the Jordan River, the Zarqa River cuts through one of the country's prime agricultural regions. Indeed, the Zarqa serves a key role in farming today, as it did in ancient times. In the Bible, this river is referred to as Jabok.

AJLUN

Long before you reach the modern mixed Moslem-Christian city of Ajlun, you will see the remains of this impressive stone fortress towering over the countryside. Don't be fooled by your first impressions: it may look like

a Crusader castle - complete with crosses carved into some of the stones - but in fact a cousin of Saleh a-Din's built it in 1185 as a defence against the advancing Latin Crusaders. The order to build it came from the regional governor, Azz el-Din Asama, but no sooner had the fortress been completed than it was no longer needed: Saleh a-Din defeated the Crusaders at the Horns of Hattin, signalling a turnaround that marked the beginning of the end of their rule in the Near East.

The crosses which are etched into the stones have an explanation. Long before the Arabs built the fortress, a monastery was located on the same site, and it was inhabited by a Christian named Ajlun. His name waskept over the centuries, and Azz el-Din Asama used some of the ruins he found when he built his defences.

In the thirteenth century, the fortress was expanded, and then it fell to the Mongols in 1260. After the Mamlukas rebuilt it, it no longer served any military purpose and became a regional administrative centre which reported directly to Damascus.

The castle commands one of the most breathtaking views in all of Jordan. On a clear day, you can see from the Sea of Galilee all the way down the Jordan Valley to the Dead Sea.

Below: *The castle stands high above the surrounding open land and villages*

GILEAD

The Land of Gilead figures prominently in a number of Bible stories. Absalom was slain while hanging by his hair from a tree in the forest of Ephraim, near Ajlun.

Elijah the prophet was said to have been born in Tishbe (I Kings 17). Most scholars agree that the town of Listib, slightly north of Ajlun, is the biblical Tishbe. Likewise, the area in which Elijah took refuge, as detailed in I Kings, is widely deemed to be in the area around Listib.

In biblical times - and as recently as the late nineteenth century - forests were plentiful in Gilead. By the end of the previous century, however, they had all but disappeared. Some attribute this severe change to the Circassians, who were settled in the region by the Turks. Whoever is to blame, however, the Jordanian government has taken on the challenge of replanting the forests that were lost.

Below: *Ajlun*

UMM QEIS (GADERA)

Perhaps best-known for the New Testament story of two evil men whose spirits were transferred by Jesus to a herd of pigs that then stampeded down a hill and into the Sea of Galilee, where they drowned (Matthew 8:28-34), Gadera has a long and proud history that includes its role as one of the more important cities of the Decapolis. It also boasts one of Jordan's more breathtaking views - of the Sea of Galilee, Golan Heights and Yarmouk River. Today, visitors can roam through the ruins of ancient Gadera, which extend over nearly a square kilometre. The black basalt and white limestone that have been used here throughout the ages make for striking scenes indeed. In Roman times, Gadera was a cultural and intellectual centre, the birthplace of the first century BC poet Meleager and many other distinctive men of letters. Just down the hill are the hot springs of Hammat Gader, and in Roman times many visitors would take the waters and then retreat up the hill to the cooler climate and the cultural offerings of Gadera.

The city had two theatres; today, the smaller of them - a 3,000 seat structure - is the better-preserved. The ancient acropolis, which sits atop a hill, is the focal point of any visit. It is surrounded by the remains of houses from the nineteenth century Ottoman town that was built here. A few years ago, the government moved the last residents into the adjacent, modern city of Umm Qeis, allowing archeologists to conduct their research more effectively. Located at the crossroads of several important trade routes, the city played an important role in commerce.

Above: *Umm Qeis, the biblical Gadera, with the Golan Heights in the background*
Overleaf Pages 42 and 43: *The antiquities of Umm Qeis, and a view of the Sea of Galilee*

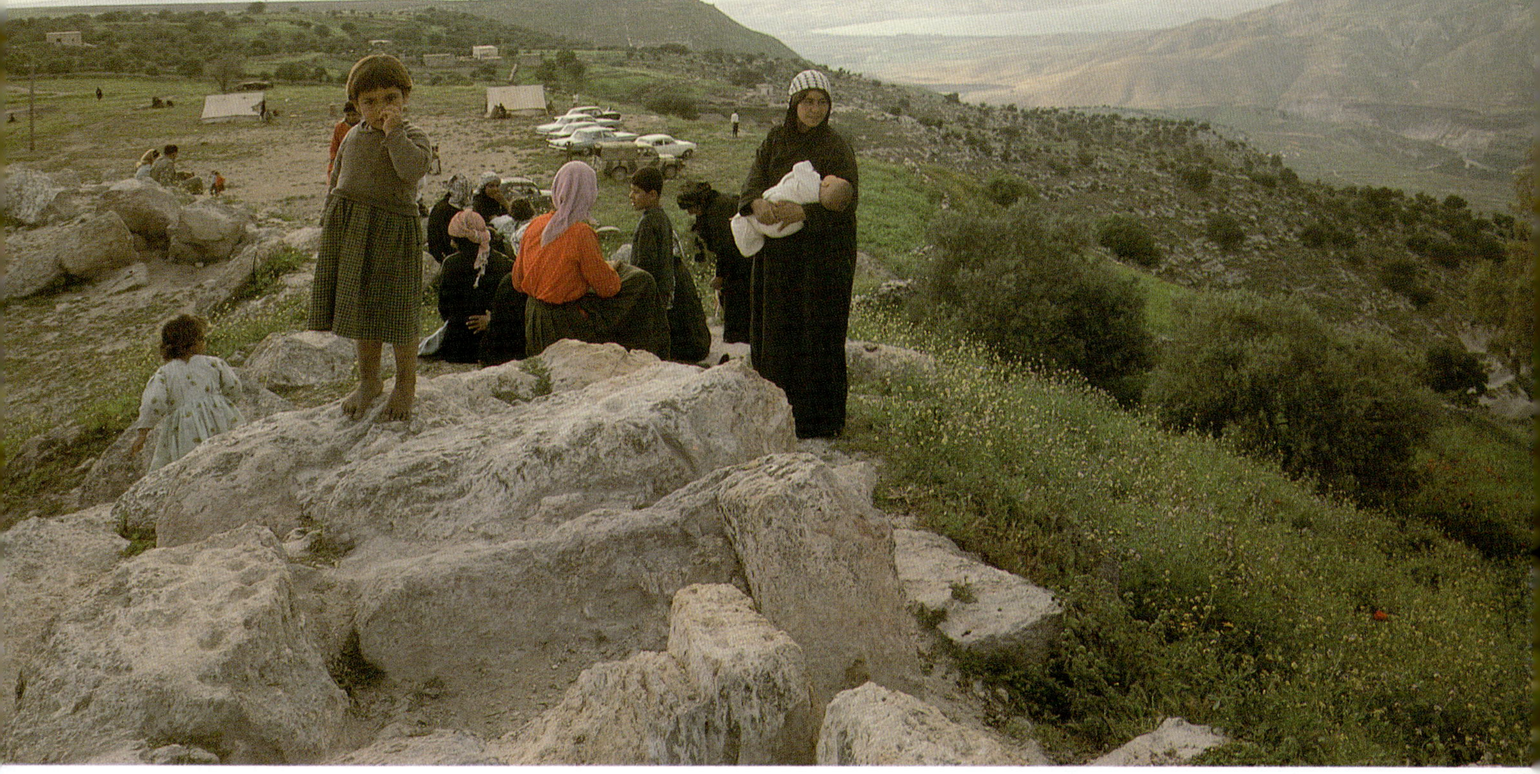

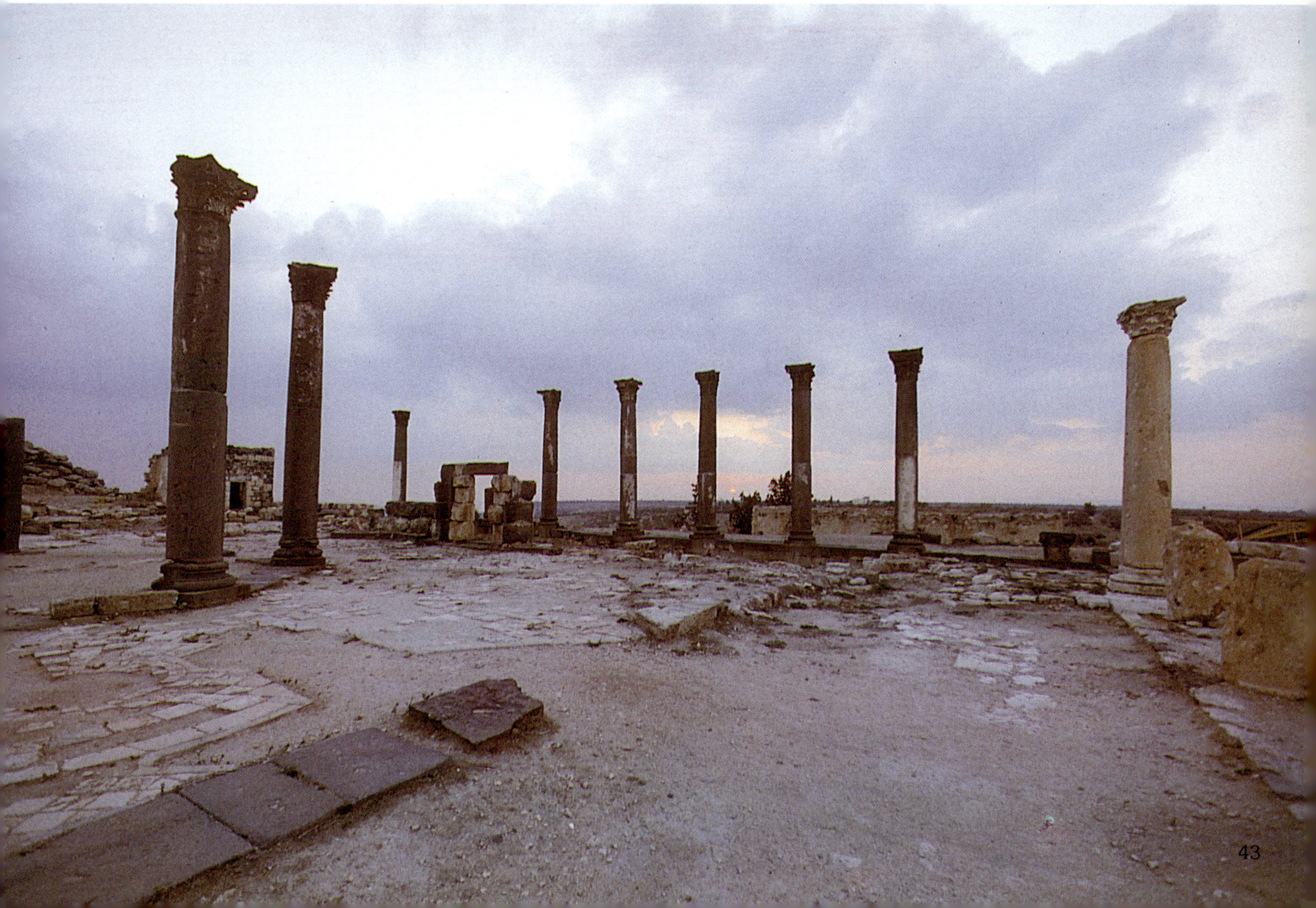

THE JORDAN VALLEY

Only one-tenth of Jordan's land area is arable. That should come as no surprise to anyone who has seen the huge expanses of desert that are so abundant in both the north and south. Thanks to natural and manmade factors, the fertile Jordan Valley is the country's No. 1 answer to the tough challenges posed by the climate.

This narrow, 100-kilometre long strip of land which lies on the border with Israel accounts for just a tiny part of Jordan's land area, but it produces 40 percent of the country's agricultural output. Thanks to excellent irrigation and use of water resources and good soil conditions, the area is home to intensive farming, especially of citrus fruit and vegetables. The irrigation projects undertaken here, which involved diverting the waters of the Yarmouk River to fields along the entire length of the Valley, have enabled the desert kingdom to create an extremely attractive agricultural zone in what otherwise was a hot, dry valley.

Throughout Jordan, the most common crop is olives, and sheep are the most common livestock. In these two fields, as in most other types of fruits and vegetables, Jordan produces more than it needs for the consumption of its own people. Home-grown wheat and beef, however, are in short supply, and the shortfall is supplemented with imports from abroad.

Above: *The Jordan Valley is the country's fertile agriculture region*

PELLA

This important historical and archeological site has been inhabited continuously for the past 6,000 years, but researchers have found many signs of life dating much further back in history: as far as one million years.

Most of the visible excavations at Pella are from the Roman, Byzantine and Islamic periods, spanning the second through fourteenth centuries AD. The truth, however, is that the area around Pella was used as either a residential or hunting and herding base during nearly every historical and prehistorical period, from the Hellenistic all the way back to the Paleolithic.

Pella is located on several important trade routes, at sea level, and adjacent to several springs which have always provided a reliable supply of fresh water. It all adds up to make this an attractive place for civilisation.

First mentioned in the literature in the nineteenth century BC, Egyptian texts called the place Pehel or Pihilum. Although no precise information has been unearthed, the city was large enough and strong enough for the Egyptians to include it in a list of enemies. At that time, it was renowned as a stop on the trade routes linking China and Arabia to Syria, Cyprus and Egypt. Apparently, the place suffered a decline, for it is not mentioned in the Bible.

In 66 AD, the Jewish rebels attacked Pella and other cities. Pella had become a refuge for many Jerusalem Christians who had fled the approaching Jews, and it became an important Christian city.

The most impressive ruins unearthed to date are those of the Civic Complex Church, so named because of its location at the heart of what was once the Roman city centre. Built in the fifth century AD by Pella's Byzantine residents, it was made of reused stones and columns from old Roman ruins in a narrow space between the odeon and the parvis.

Later, it was one of the ten cities of the Decapolis, along with nearby Jerash, Scythopolis (today Beit Shean, west of the Jordan River) and others.

Below: *View through an archway of Pella*

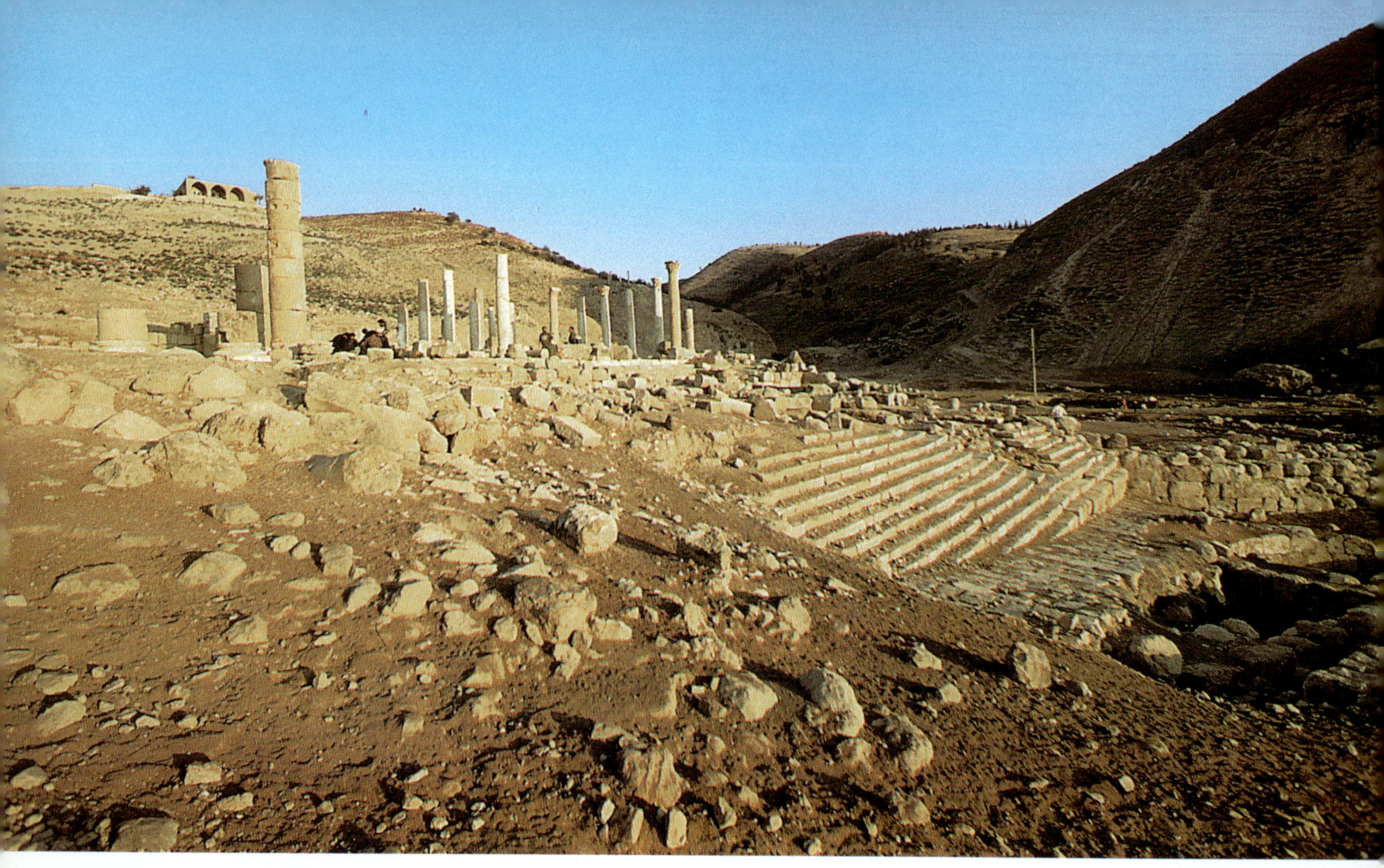

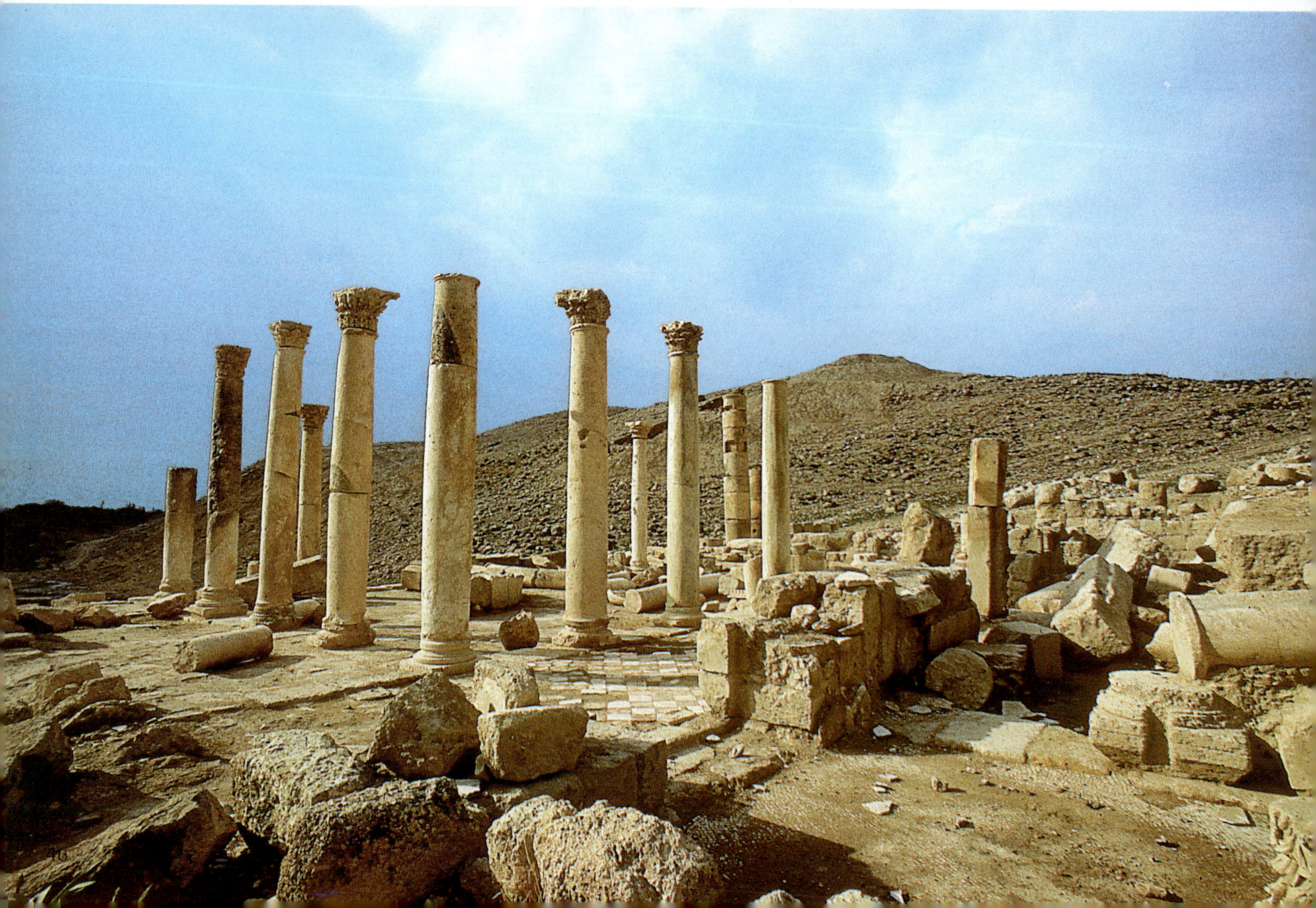

The Arab conquest turned Pella into an Umayyad city in the seventh century, and some beautiful ceramic remains have been uncovered here. The city seems to have prospered until 747, when the earthquake that levelled so much of Jordan did not spare Pella.

Far Left: *The monumental staircase leading to the Civic Complex Church*
Left: *Roman columns reused by the Byzantines to build their churches*
Below Left: *Roman columns recently restored by the Jordanian Antiquities Department*
Below: *Excavations reveal Umayyad housing from the seventh or eighth century*

UMM EL-JIMAL

Although only about 100 millimetres of rain fall here each year, Roman, Byzantine and Umayyad settlers all used sophisticated water collection, storage and irrigation techniques to cultivate wheat and vegetables.

First settled by the Nabateans in the first century BC as part of their expansion northwards, by the second century AD it had been incorporated into the Roman Province of Arabia. It prospered, and had a resident population of 2,000 – 3,000 people, until it fell victim to the turmoil that jolted much of the region in the third century and was destroyed. In the fourth and fifth centuries, the area was repopulated, but this time primarily as a military outpost - one small component of an intricate defense system set up by Emperors Diocletian and Constantine. Later still, in the fifth and sixth centuries, it was rebuilt as a prosperous trading and farming outpost. Its fortunes were waning, however, by the eighth century, and the devastation of the 747 earthquake caused its residents to abandon it. Only at the beginning of the twentieth century was any further attempt made to settle Umm el-Jimal. A group of Druze

lived here briefly, before continuing south to Amman. Umm el-Jimal is impressive precisely because it lacks the monumental structures found in ancient Philadelphia, Jerash and other Roman cities. Its ruins reveal black basalt buildings that were home to farmers and shepherds. Many of the remains reach two and even three storeys into the still sky. The labyrinthian walls seem to extend in every direction with no overall plan. Doorways connect separate houses and the remains of stairways lead up and down. Around 1950, a modern city began to sprout up around the ancient ruins.

Above Left: *Remains of a two-storey house made of basalt in Umm el-Jimal*
Left: *Arches of the West Church*
Above: *Byzantine barracks were built in Umm el-Jimal in the fifth century*

some actually were built on ruins left behind by the Romans. While some of them did serve as castles of sorts, others were hunting lodges, farming complexes or pleasure getaway points for the caliphs who longed for the desert life instead of the city routine in Damascus.

The castles may have had political significance, as the desert dwellers of Jordan were among the strongest supporters of the Umayyad rulers in Damascus. Indeed, when everyone around them revolted against Damascus in 660-670 AD, they remained loyal. Some scholars suggest that the castles may be an expression of this two-way loyalty and trust.

A visit to the desert castles can take a day or more. With a refreshing stop at the Rest House at Azraq, it can be an enjoyable way to glimpse into life at the edge of the desert.

THE DESERT CASTLES

East of Amman, just as you begin to feel as if you have left all civilisation behind, the Umayyad Desert Castles spring into view. But not all were built by the Umayyads, and not all of them were truly castles. Nonetheless, the name has stuck to this impressive collection of desert outposts.

Some were built in the style of Roman fortresses. Indeed,

QASR EL-HALLABAT

Originally built as a small Roman fort in the early second century AD, Qasr el-Hallabat was expanded in the third century and renovated in the sixth century. In the Umayyad period, the entire structure was dismantled and rebuilt in accordance with its original plan. Additional structures were built, including a bathhouse, a mosque and a network of dams, reservoirs and irrigation systems.

The rebuilt main building was decorated with beautiful mosaics and frescos that featured floral and geometric designs, as well as representations of animals and human beings. (The early Moslems were less concerned with such representations than their successors would be.)

Many of the stones used to rebuild the fortress carry parts of Greek inscriptions. The Umayyads used them as regular building blocks, without any regard for what was written on them. In many cases, the writing appears upside down or sideways. In no instance was an entire inscription preserved.

The nearby bathhouse is a well-preserved structure called Hammam es-Sarah, which the Umayyads also decorated ornately.

Left Above: *Umayyad mosaic floor*
Left Below: *Aerial view of Qasr el-Hallabat*
Below: *The mosque at Qasr el-Hallabat*
Above: *A camel in the desert*

AZRAQ

In prehistoric times, this area was covered by a huge lake. More recently, its year-round springs and bodies of water have made Azraq an important oasis and rest stop on trade routes.

The fort itself, which measures 80 by 70 metres, was one of a series of Roman defencive positions drawn through the desert. Little is known about the structure, other than the fact that it was built by the Romans in the late third or early fourth centuries AD, as indicated by an inscription that dedicates it to Emperors Diocletian and Maximilian. Azraq lies at the meeting point of the basalt-laden desert and Wadi Sirhan, which stretches south to Saudi Arabia. Through the ages, salt mining has been a major source of income for the people of the region.

The Roman architecture includes massive basalt doors whose pivoting hinges are built as an integral part of the doors themselves. Some of these doors survive to this day.

Azraq was an important military outpost for the Romans, and for the Byzantines who came after them. The Umayyad caliphs were drawn to the place in the seventh and eighth centuries because of the abundant wildlife population in the oasis. They were avid hunters, and Azraq offered them a veritable year-round playground.

But Azraq's military career was far from over. In 1237, the fortress was rebuilt by the Ayyubids, shortly after Saleh a-Din had driven the last of the Crusaders from Jerusalem and the area east of the Jordan River.

Nearly 300 years later, in 1516, the Ottomans used Azraq as a garrison. Then, in 1917, T. E. Lawrence (Lawrence of Arabia) set up his headquarters here when he and the great-grandfather of King Hussein, Sherif Hussein of Mecca, led the Arab Revolt against the Ottomans.

Below: Outside the fortress at Azraq
Right: Beyond the fortress walls lies a rich and lush oasis

Today, thanks to heavy pumping of the area's water resources to quench the nation's thirst, the oasis at Azraq is a mere shadow of its former self. The millions of migrating birds that used to stop here as they traversed Asia and Africa have found other stopping points.

Left: *Preparing traditional Beduin coffee in the desert*
Below: *Outside the fortress at Azraq*
Above Right: *The oasis at Azraq is home to many varieties of birds and wildlife*
Below Right: *The Azraq Rest House*

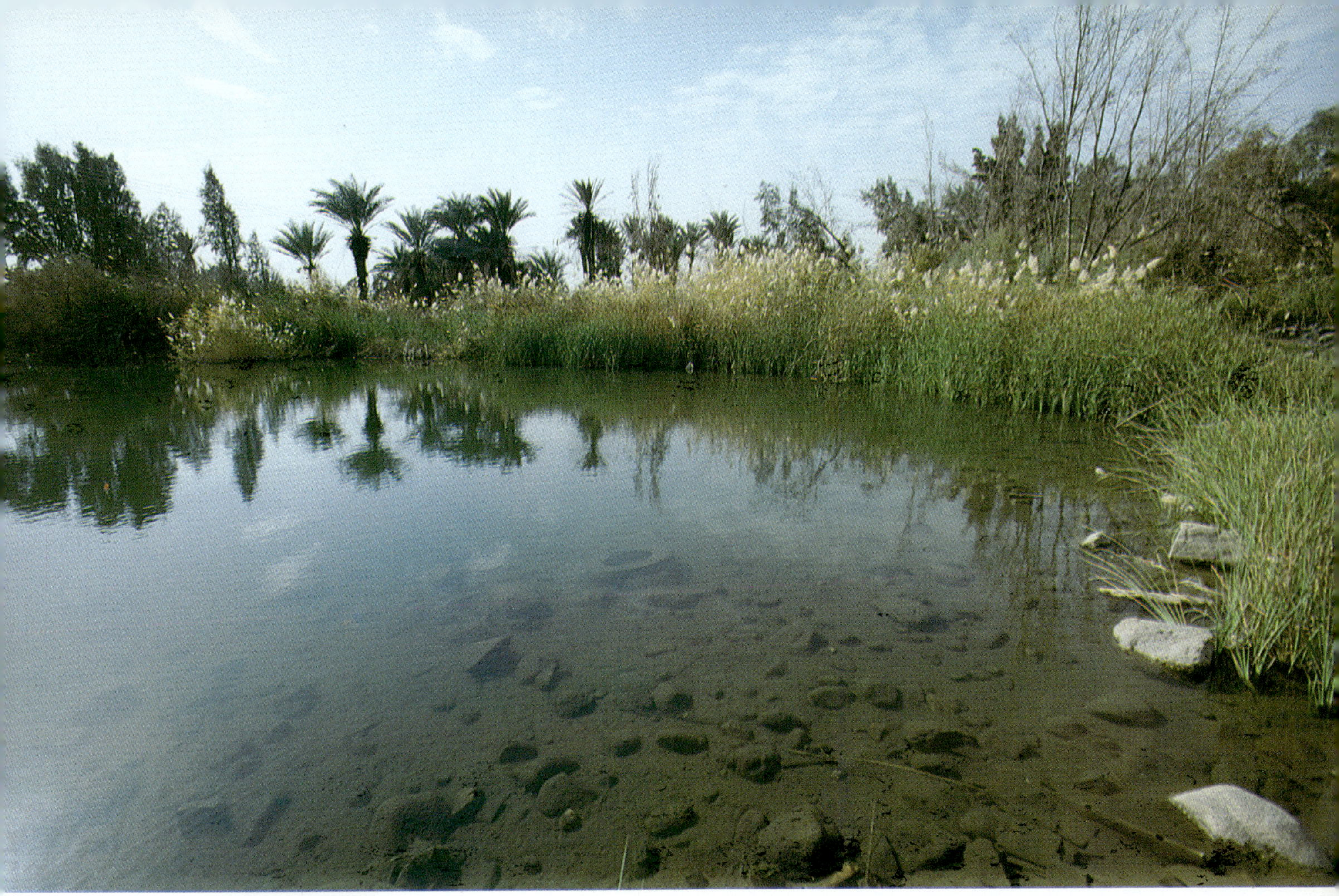

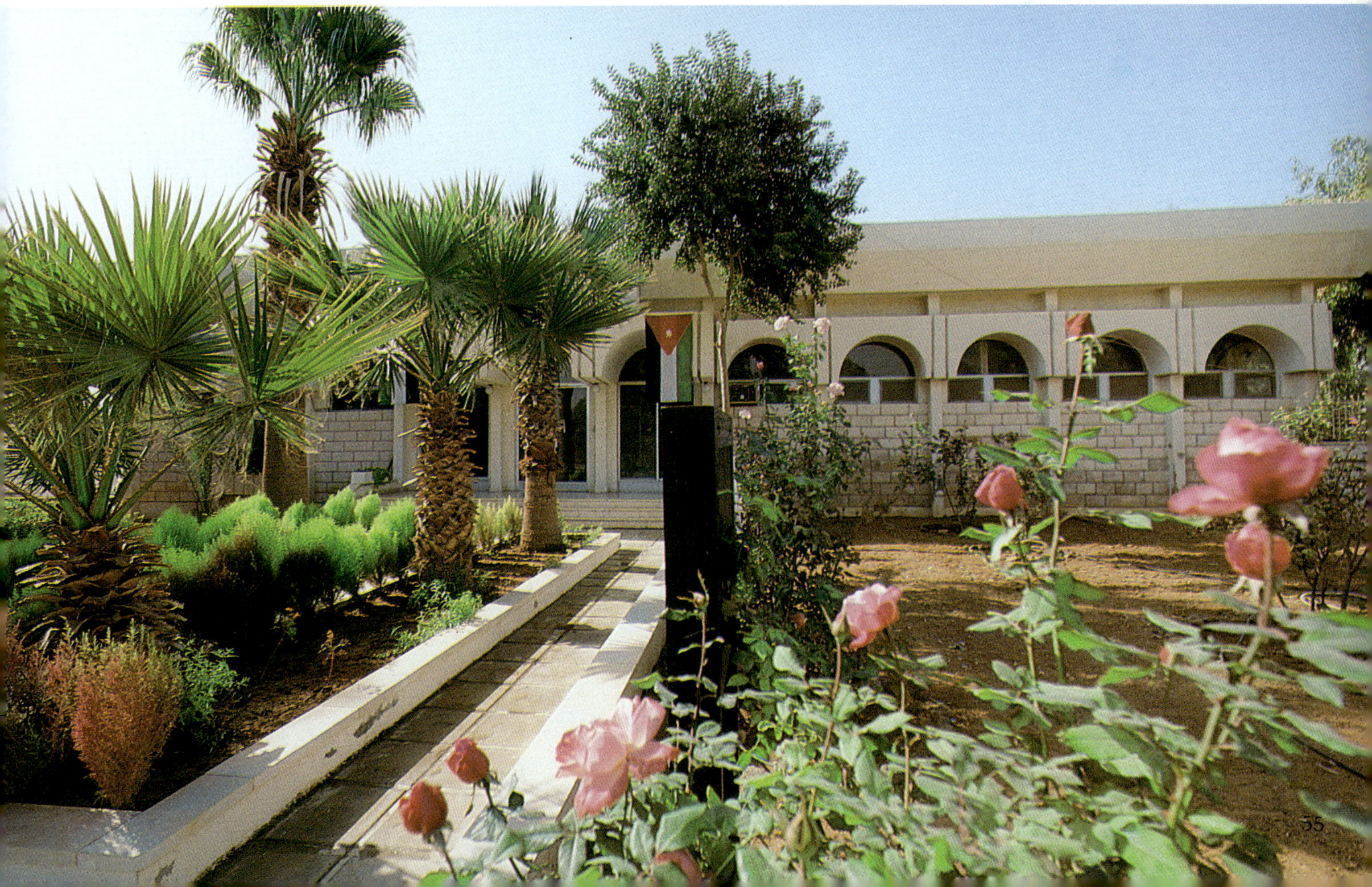

Above: The Desert Castle at Amra
Above Right: Detail of frescos in Qasr Amra
Right: Dome of the Calidarium
Far Right: Inside the audience hall

QASR AMRA

Here, some 85 kilometres east of Amman, lies what is probably Jordan's finest Umayyad Desert Castle. The walls and ceilings of this complex are covered with vivid frescos that provide what has been described as one of the best glimpses at early Arab art.

The Koran does not forbid depicting human and animal faces in art, but later religious writings make the ban clear and total. These frescos were completed before the order came forbidding graven images and, for reasons that we cannot know, the castle was spared the treatment that befell so many other frescos in the Moslem world. The scenes remain untouched, albeit worn away by time, the elements and centuries of neglect.

The complex looks unassuming from outside. The main building, an audience hall, has three parallel barrel vaults and a couple of small anterooms. The bathhouse consists of three small rooms. Scholars believe that the buildings

visitors see today may be just the last remaining element of a much larger complex that could have included a fortress, a dam and an enclosed farming area of 25 hectares.

The site offers no clear evidence as to when it was constructed, but in all likelihood it was completed during the reign of either Caliph Walid I (705-715 AD) or his uncle, Caliph Walid II (743-744.)

The first Moslem injunction against human images in art was issued between 720-724 by Caliph Yazid II, but as noted, the frescos at Qasr Amra survived.

The frescos depict a variety of scenes that were typical of Umayyad art: men on horseback chasing animals into net traps; naked bathing women; bathing children and women; men exercising outdoors; reclining women flanked by peacocks; dancing women; and more.

The audience hall's walls also are decorated by portraits of four "enemies of Islam" who were conquered by Walid I: the Byzantine Emperor; the Visgoth King of Spain; the Sassanian Emperor; and Negus of Abyssinia.

DOME OF THE CALIDARIUM

The small, domed ceiling of the calidarium, or hot room, is decorated by a fresco of the heavens. Along with the signs of the Zodiac, it contains a depiction of the stars seen in the Northern Hemisphere. This is the earliest known example of a depiction of the heavens that was presented on a round - not flat - surface.

Left and Above: *Close-ups of the frescos that adorn the walls and ceilings at Qasr Amra*

QASR KHARANA

One scholar called Qasr Kharana "probably the best-preserved of the Umayyad desert castles, and the least understood." More than any of the other "castles," this one looks very much the part of a castle fortress. Looks, however, can be deceiving; it was not used as a defensive post. One theory holds that it may have been a meeting place where politicians from the area could hold gatherings, but nobody is sure.

Inside the thick walls of the 35 metre square building are 61 rooms on two floors. The lack of ceilings in some of the upstairs rooms indicates that construction was never finished. A painted inscription indicates that Walid I's entourage stopped here on the way back from Mecca in 710 AD.

Right: *The arched entryway*
Below: *Beduin caretaker outside Qasr Kharana*

QASR MUSHATTA

The orange bricks of this never-completed castle make a striking impression just outside Amman's Queen Alia International Airport. Ground probably was broken around 743 AD by Caliph Walid II, but the Umayyad rule gave way to the Abbasids before it could be completed.

Signs of splendour are found everywhere amid the ruins: arches, intricately carved stones, toppled columns, the remains of a luxurious throne room and mosque. Had it been completed and preserved, Qasr Mushatta would have offered one of the best glimpses at Umayyad craftsmanship and design.

Left: *Entrance to Qasr Kharana*
Below: *Aerial view shows the castle next to the airport*

THE DEAD SEA

At 400 metres below sea level, the Dead Sea is the lowest point on earth. The water's high salt and mineral content makes even nonswimmers float in the warm, briny fluid. And, being so far below sea level, the sun's dangerous rays are filtered out before they reach bathers on the beach!

The Dead Sea has long been an important industrial region for Jordan, which exports ample quantities of phosphates and minerals drawn from the area. Its proximity to Madaba, Mt. Nebo and other tourism sites has helped it become an increasingly popular draw in its own right.

DOLMENS

North of the Dead Sea, the Jordan Valley is dotted with these mysterious ancient stone structures. Generally comprising four thick standing stone slabs with a fifth slab lying on top, they also are found in Europe and elsewhere in the Middle East. Nobody knows their significance. Jordan's largest concentrations of dolmens are found in Damieh, el-Quttein and Matabi, although smaller numbers are located in Jerash and elsewhere.

Left: *The Dead Sea*
Right: *Salt 'pillars' and accumulation of minerals floating on the southern part of the Dead Sea.*
Above: *A dolmen*
Below: *Sunset over the Dead Sea, as seen from Mt. Nebo*

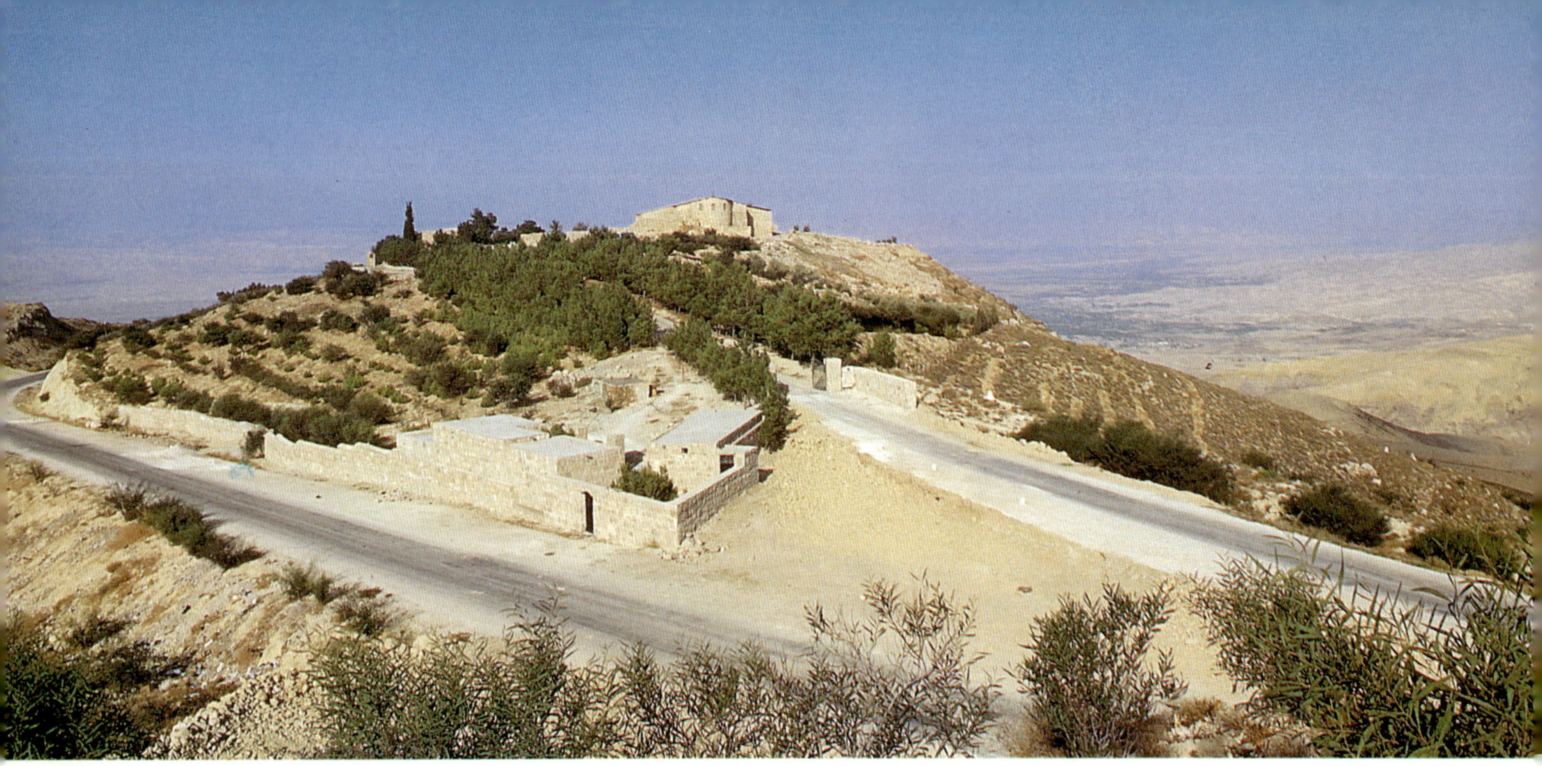
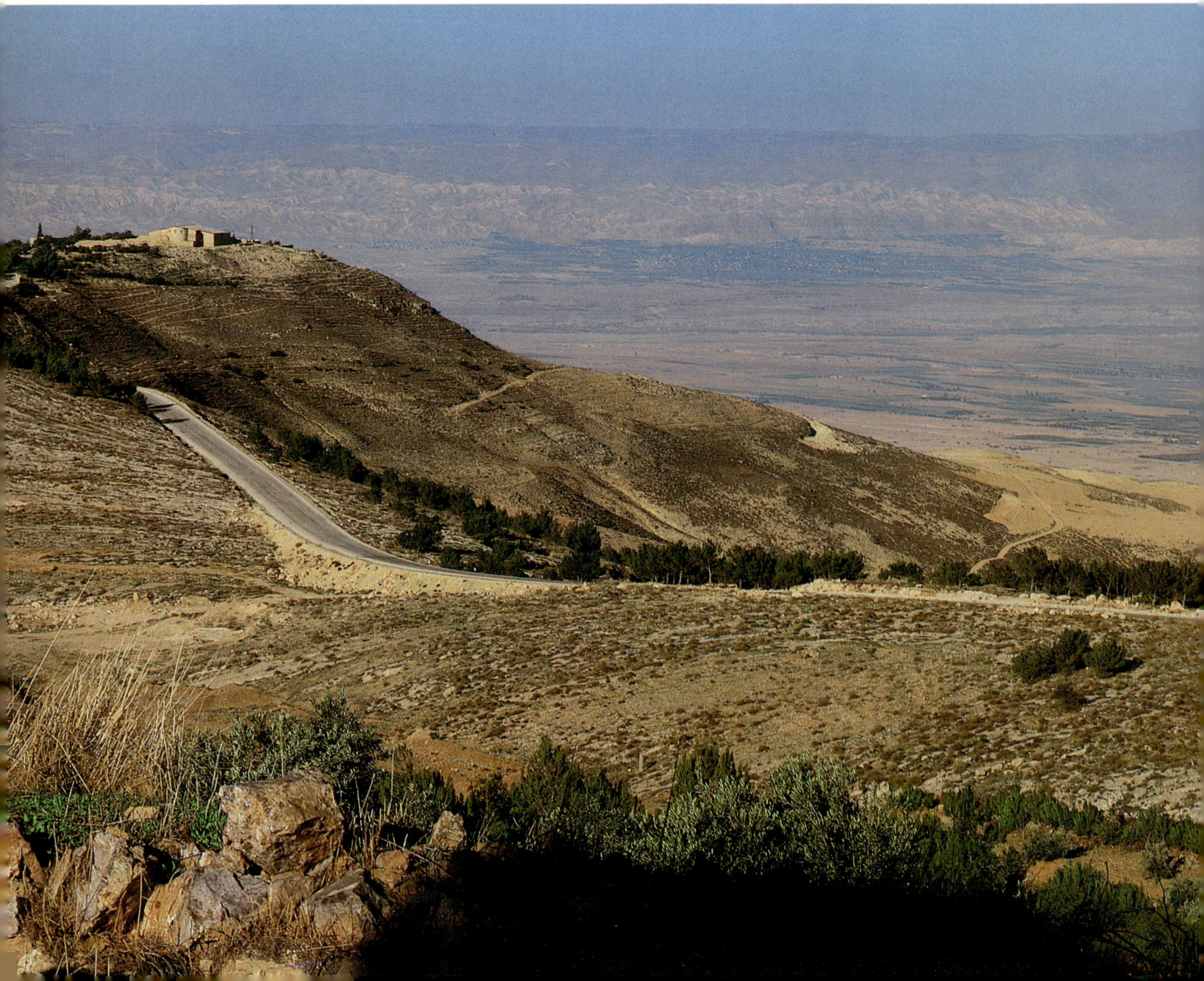

MT. NEBO

Here Moses stood and gazed over Canaan, the Promised Land. After leading his people through the desert for 40 years, the Book of Deuteronomy recounts, God forbade him from setting foot on the longed-for soil.

From 800 metres above sea level, Mt. Nebo commands a breathtaking view of all that Moses saw but could not touch. On a clear day, visitors can see the Judean hills, the Dead Sea and Jerusalem.

In Deuteronomy 34, we learn that Moses died here. A number of churches and memorials have been built here over the ages. The first was built in the fourth century on the presumed site of Moses' death. In the sixth century, a basilica was built with beautiful mosaic floors depicting hunting scenes.

In the late sixth century, the church was expanded and remodelled extensively. Worshippers were greeted with an optimistic sign reading: "Peace to everybody."

A monastery housing the monks who lived here for centuries also stands atop Mt. Nebo.

Extensive excavations in the past century - led by the Franciscan Archeological Institute - have revealed numerous mosaic floors that adorned churches, stores and private homes. The Madaba School of mosaics is an important part of Jordan's art history.

The Franciscan monks live in a modern monastery that stands alongside the excavations of the old one.

Left and Below: *Mt. Nebo commands a breathtaking view of the Judean hills, all the way to Jerusalem. At its peak is the church and monastery complex*
Next Pages:
Left: *Mosaic in the Baptistry of Moses, Mt. Nebo*
Right: *Mosaic floor of the Church of Saints Lot and Procopius*

Above: *City view*
Left: *Church of St. George*
Right: *Section of the Madaba Map depicting Jerusalem*

MADABA

Over a span of 3,500 years, Madaba has alternately been an important focal point of history and an abandoned pile of ruins. The Israelites conquered it (Numbers 21:30, Joshua 13:9-16), and King David's army defeated the Ammonites and Arameans here (I Chronicles 19:7-19.) In the ninth century BC, it was retaken by the King of Moab, Mesha.

But that was not the end of the battles over and in Madaba. The Maccabees were attacked and fought here, and it was ruled by Jews and others over the centuries until the Nabatean King Aretas III won it back in the first century BC.

Christianity came to the area in the early centuries AD, and most of what is known about Madaba from that period has been gleaned from the spectacular mosaics and fragments that have been excavated.

ΑΓΡΟΙΚΙϹ ΕΡΩϹ ΧΑΡΙϹ ΕΡΩϹ ΧΑΡΙϹ ΧΑΡΙϹ ΕΡΩϹ ΑΦΡΟΔΙΤΗ ΑΔΩΝΙϹ ΕΡΩϹ

ΘΕΡΑΠΕΝΑΙ ΦΑΙΔΡΑ ΠΡΟΠΟΛΟΙ ΙΠΠΟΛΥΤΟϹ ΔΟΥΛΟϹ

Above Left: *Excavations in Madaba*
Above: *Detail of mosaic in Church of the Apostles*
Below Left: *Detail from the Byzantine Hyppolytus Hall, excavated beneath the Church of the Virgin*
Below Centre: *Detail of mosaic in Church of the Apostles*

Below Right: *Medallion depicting lamb eating leaves of a tree, the Twal Family Chapel*
Overleaf:
Left: *Personification of the Sea, Church of the Apostles*
Below: *Shepherd tends his flock on the outskirts of Madaba*

THE MADABA MAP

In 1898, while construction crews were building a Greek Orthodox church on the site of an ancient Byzantine church, they stumbled upon the sixth century map of Palestine that has made Madaba famous. It depicts the Holy Land, from Alexandria in the south to Sidon in the north, and from the Mediterranean Sea in the west to the deserts east of Amman. At the centre of the map, which measured 25 metres by 5.6 metres (today only 15.7 metres survive) is a detailed map of Jerusalem, and at the heart of the map of Jerusalem lies the Church of the Holy Sepulchre.

Comprised of an estimated 2.3 million tiles, it must have taken some 11,500 hours to assemble. Almost 150 sites are labelled in colour-coded tile, and most of them have been identified. Today, visitors can see the map in the yellow brick Greek Orthodox Church of St. George.

Accelerated excavation work has uncovered an impressive array of mosaics and fragments in the city, causing many to call it the City of Mosaics. Other impressive mosaics can be seen in the Madaba Archeological Museum, the Church of the Apostles and other excavation sites.

Madaba was levelled by the 747 earthquake, and it lay abandoned for more than 1,000 years. In 1880, 2,000 Christians from Kerak settled among the ruins. Today, it is a large, modern, mainly Christian city.

ZARQA MA'IN

The hot springs at Zarqa Ma'in and nearby Ain ez Zara provided relief from rheumatism for Herod the Great during the last years of his life. In Genesis 36:24, references to the hot springs discovered by the first kings of Edom probably refer to these springs.

The hot springs and sulfer springs in the area have made Zarqa Ma'in a popular destination for rest and relaxation. The naturally hot waters cascade down impressive waterfalls and mix together with cold water, in season, before flowing into the Dead Sea.

Particularly in springtime, the area hotels are filled, and thousands of people bathe in the covered and uncovered pools.

Left and Below: *Cascading waterfalls and hot springs make the hotels at Zarqa Ma'in a popular destination*

MUKAWIR (MACHAERUS)

John the Baptist was put to death here, his punishment for protesting the decision of Herod's son Herod Antipas to divorce his Nabatean wife and take his brother's wife as his own.

The Hasmonean ruler Alexander Jannaeus (103-76 BC) built a fortress here to protect his territory against the Nabateans. The Nabateans never conquered the site, but the Romans did - in 63 BC.

Herod restored the fortress, turning it into what Josephus Flavius called "a palace, breathtaking in size and beauty." When Jerusalem fell to the Romans in 70 AD, many Jews sought refuge in Machaerus, which was ultimately destroyed two years later.

The modern town, called Mukawir, is inhabited by Beduin who have suffered from economic woes for many years. Since 1985, a local project employing Beduin women in the traditional craft of rug weaving has helped improve the situation. The colourful carpets they produce, in traditional and modern designs, are sold locally and abroad.

QASR EL MISHNEQEH

Half an hour's walk from Mukawir, high atop a mountain peak, is Qasr el Mishneqeh, the site of the fortress and a huge reservoir for storing rainwater. The name, which means Citadel of the Gallows, stems from the fact that here John the Baptist was killed.

Above Left: Excavations at Machaerus
Below Left and Far Left: A return to traditional Beduin weaving has breathed new life into the area
Below: Aerial view of Qasr el Mishneqeh

AYOUN MOUSA

The Springs of Moses, so named because Moses is believed to be buried in the area, provide water to Madaba. Evidence of a long history of habitation can be seen in the dolmens, flint tools and tombs in the area. An Iron Age fortress, el-Meshhad, stands near the springs.

UMM RASAS

This fortified complex surrounded by high walls contains a 14-metre tower that may have been used as a watch-tower or as a meditation platform for the monks.
The outstanding "find" in Umm Rasas is the impressive, well-preserved mosaic in the Church of St. Stephen, completed in 785 AD. The mosaic, which was excavated in 1986, depicts renderings of Jerusalem, Kastron Mefaa (as Umm Rasas was called then) and 26 other towns in Palestine, Transjordan and the Egyptian Delta.

Left: *Ayoun Mousa*
Above: *The tower at Umm Rasas*
Right: *Aerial view of Umm Rasas*

Bottom: *General view of the mosaic at the Church of St. Stephen*
Below and Left: *Closeups of animals in the mosaic*
Opposite Page: *Closeups of four of the towns depicted in the mosaic at the Church of St. Stephen (from Top Left, clockwise): Jerusalem, Madaba, Gaza, Caesarea*

WADI MUJIB (ARNON)

Wadi Mujib, the biblical Arnon River, flows at the bottom of a 400 metre deep, four kilometre wide crevice created by an earthquake. In biblical times, the river was the boundary between the Amorites in the north and the Moabites in the south.

MOAB

South of Amman and east of the Dead Sea lie the hills of Moab, the scene of many biblical adventures. It was here that Moses gazed over the land that God would not let him enter, and it was here that David sought refuge when he was on the run from Saul.

The hills make for striking, beautiful scenery, and the presence of Wadi Mujib, Mt. Nebo and other important sites makes this area an important stop on any visitor's itinerary.

Near Right, Far Right and Below: *Wadi Mujib*
Below Right: *Wadi Zarqa*
Below Far Right: *Roman milestones*

KERAK

Although it is mentioned (by several names, including Kir Haraseth) as far back as the Iron Age, and Isaiah even prophesied its destruction, Kerak achieved prominence only after the Crusaders built a fortress here.

In 1142, the castle was completed, and Kerak was made capital of the province. Thanks to its strategic location along the King's Highway, Kerak was well-placed to play an active role in trade.

Over the centuries, the castle has been fought over, and handed back and forth between the Arabs, Mamluks, Ottomans, local individuals, the British and, finally, the Jordanians. The Mamluks and the Ottomans added annexes to the fortress castle, but it remains an excellent example of Crusader architecture - probably the most impressive in the line of Crusader castles that dot the landscape from Turkey to southern Jordan. The underground rooms served as barracks; the above-ground rooms are long, narrow halls with small slits for windows. The complex is surrounded by a deep dry moat - to which prisoners were cast for certain death.

Right and Below: Karak's Crusader castle commands a breathtaking view of the area

WADI ARABA

Extending 180 kilometres south of the Dead Sea to the Red Sea port city of Aqaba, Wadi Araba offers striking desert landscapes and a surprising number of terrain changes.

While the Dead Sea is 400 metres below sea level, Wadi Araba quickly climbs to as high as 280 metres above sea level. Along the way from the Dead Sea to the Red Sea, visitors can stop at several archeological excavations, including a remarkably preserved copper mining and smelting centre at Wadi Finan.

Above: Wadi Araba offers beautiful desert scenery
Below: View of the Dead Sea from Wadi Safi.In the background is the mountaintop fortress of Masada

SHOBAK

The Shobak Crusader castle stands a bit north of Petra, just off the old Roman Road. It was built by King Baldwin I in 1115 at a strategic high point that assured whoever occupied it control of the area's trade routes. After attacking it several times, Saleh a-Din finally took the castle in 1189. In the thirteenth century, the Mamluks conquered it and renovated extensively.

The outer walls still stand, but inside, little of the room division remains to be seen. The most interesting element: a seemingly endless staircase with 375 steps leading deep down into the earth to the castle's water reserves.

Below: Crusader castle at Shobak
Opposite Page:
Top: *The Forum Hotel at the entrance to Petra*
Middle: *Shops at Wadi Mousa*
Bottom: *Modern city of Wadi Mousa, adjacent to Petra*

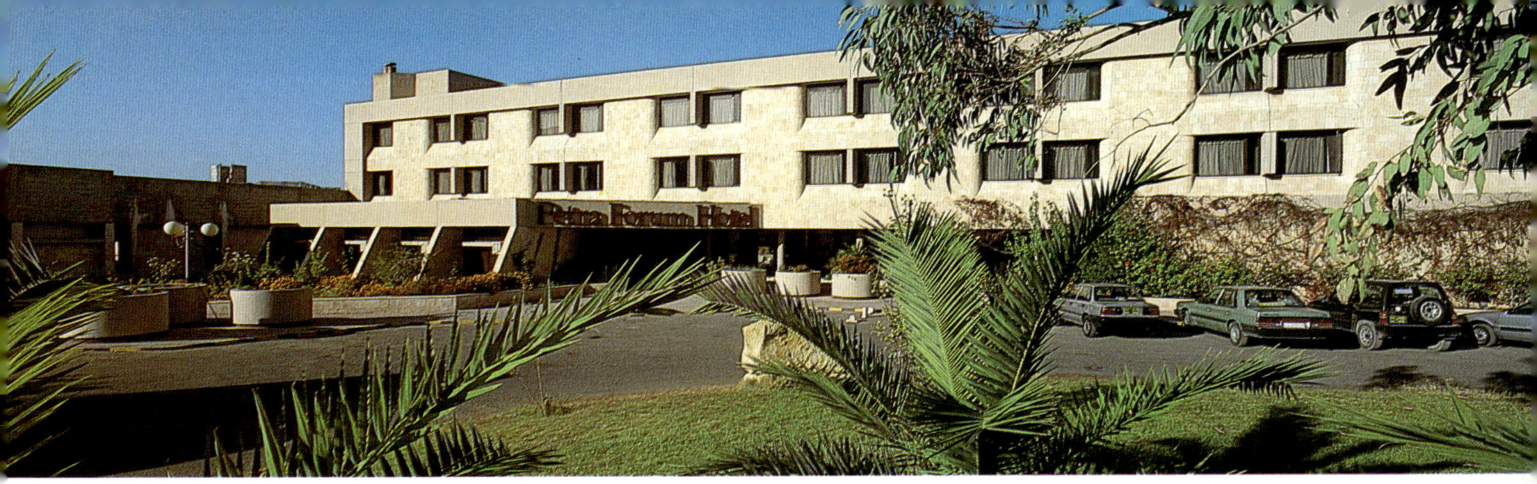
Petra Forum Hotel

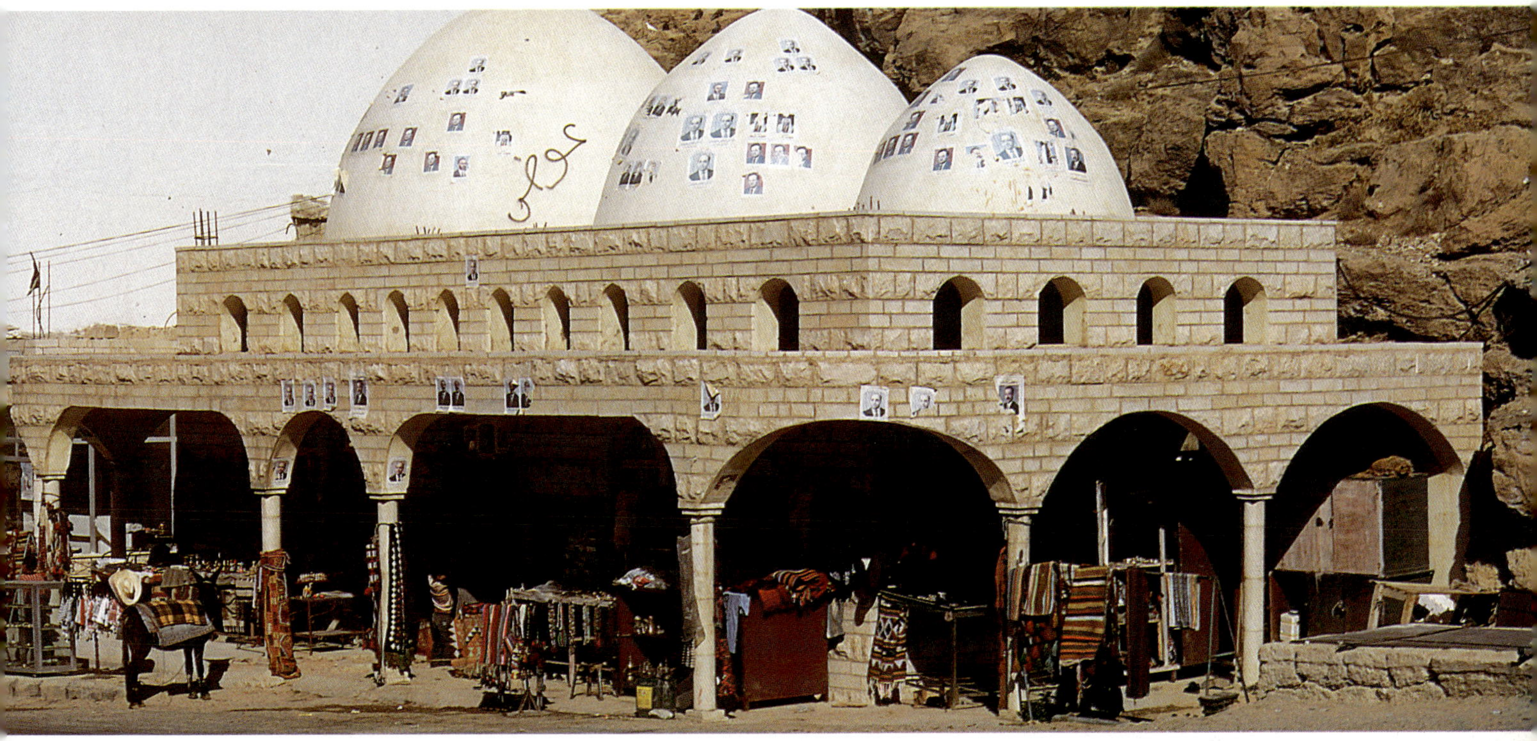

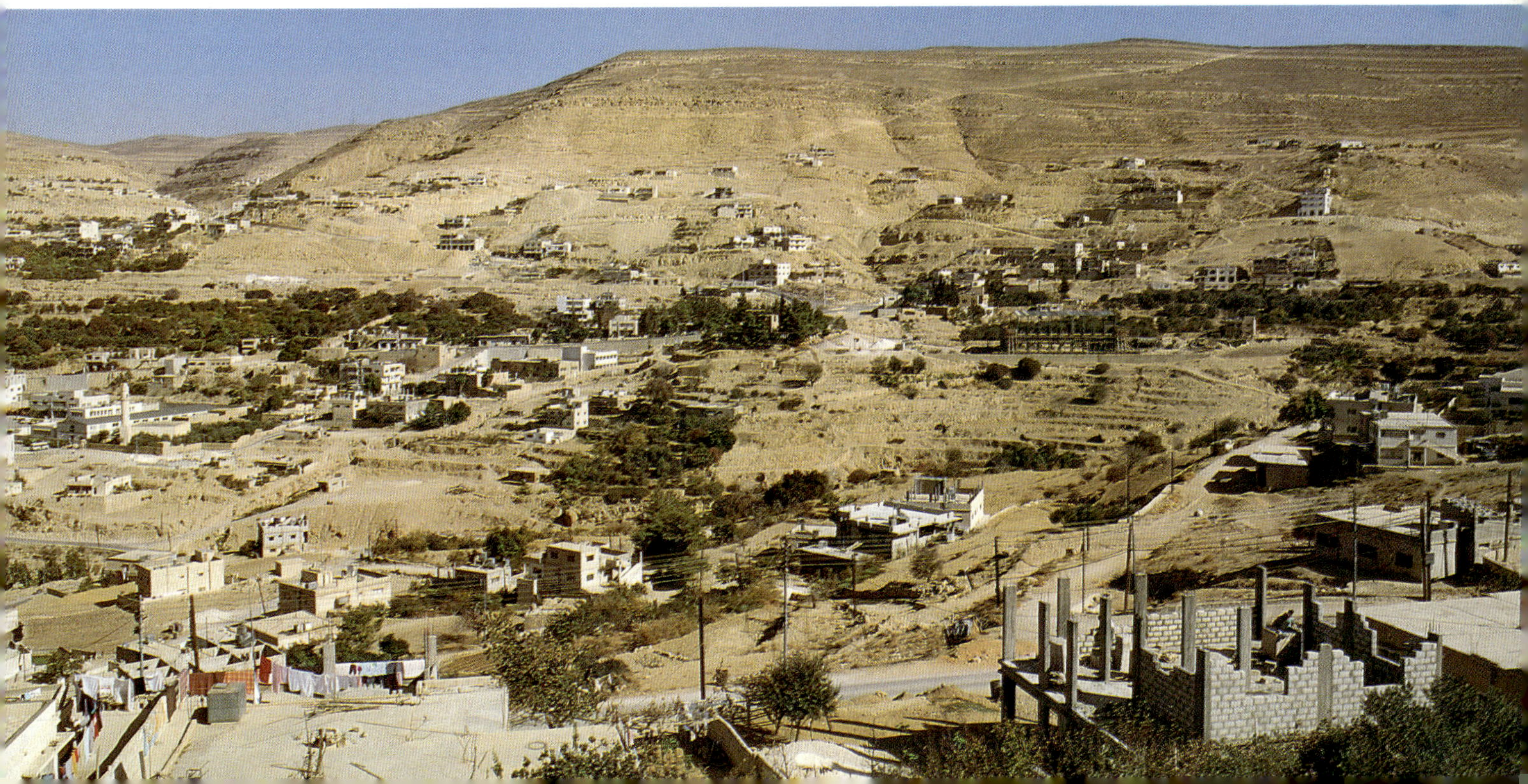

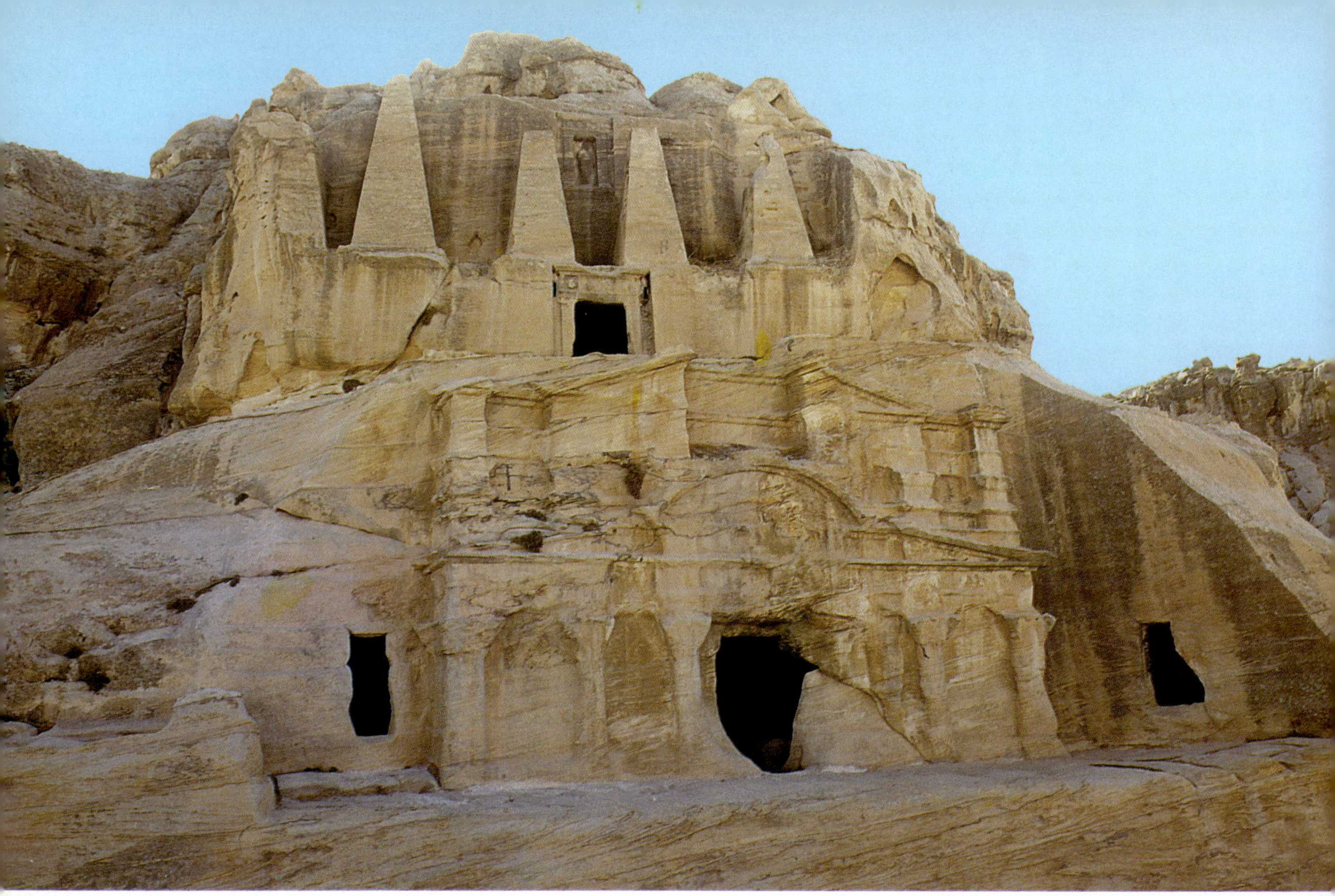

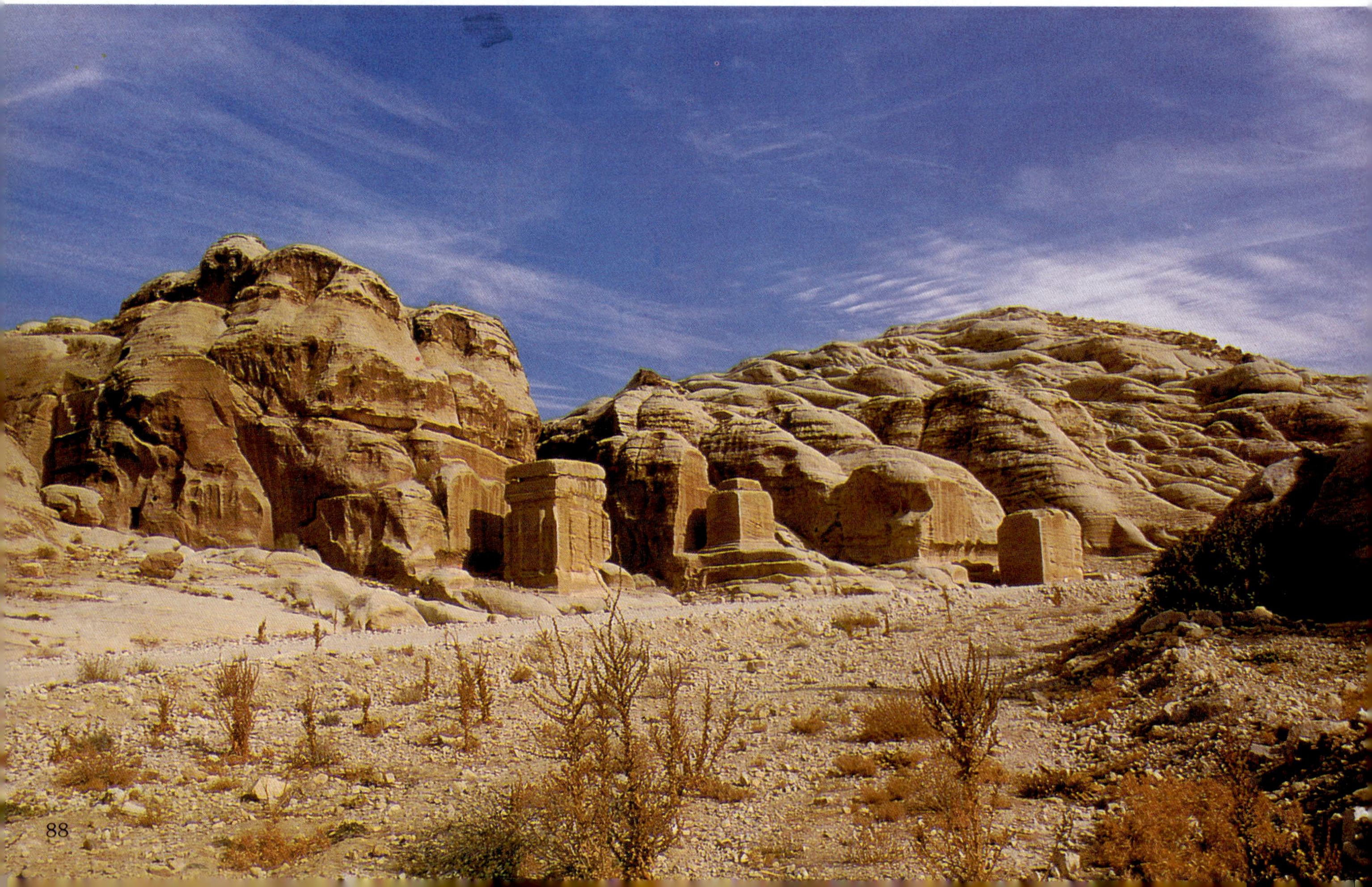

PETRA

No site in Jordan captures the visitor's imagination and takes his breath away as dramatically as Petra. The amount of labour involved in carrying the magnificent structures in the colourful soft rock boggles the mind. When first-time visitors learn that all of the structures they see were burial places, and that the Nabateans' housing did not survive, many cannot hide their bewilderment.

The Nabateans first came here in the sixth century BC, and for many years their capital was here. They gained control of lucrative trade routes and carved their edifices into the coloured stone at Petra (which actually means "stone" in ancient Greek.) Among the legends about the place, one holds that when Moses struck a rock and drew water (Exodus 17), it was here, in a place that has come to be called, appropriately, Ayoun Mousa, or Moses' Spring.

The Nabateans enjoyed centuries of prosperity in their city of stone, and maintained a sort of coexistence with

Far Left: *The Obelisk Tomb and Bab es-Siq Tricinium*
Left: *Riding into the Siq*
Bottom Left: *The mysterious Djin blocks*
Below: *Niche monument in the Siq with two featureless god representations*

the Romans long after the latter had gained control over most of the region. In 106 AD, however, the Romans took over Petra as well. Earthquakes in 363 and 747 caused severe damage, and Petra was cut off from the West for over 1,000 years. The Beduin who lived among the stones guarded their secret place jealously, refusing entry to outsiders.

Then, in 1812, a young Swiss explorer named Johann Ludwig Burckhardt took on the alias of a devout Moslem named Ibrahim ibn Abdullah and entered Petra. He told his suspicious guide that he had vowed to sacrifice a goat at Jabal Haroun (Mt. Aaron, where the Beduin believe that Moses' brother died and is buried.)

Burckhardt's accounts of Petra were published in Europe, and slowly, inevitably, the ancient city opened to outsiders once again.

The local Beduin - who lived in the rock tombs of Petra until the mid-1980s, when the Jordanian government moved the last of them to neighbouring Wadi Mousa - have long since overcome their distaste for foreigners. Today, they welcome visitors wholeheartedly and go out of their way to be hospitable.

THE SIQ

The passage into Petra begins with a walk or a ride through the narrow passageway of more than one kilometre in length. On each side of the dirt path, brilliantly coloured rock rises toward the heavens. The closer you get to the Treasury, the more vivid the shades of red, orange and pink seem to become.

THE TREASURY

Nobody knows why the first facade cut into stone that greets people as they emerge from the Siq is called the Treasury; many things about Petra remain a mystery, but have no doubt about it: this building was always a burial site and never had anything to do with money matters. The well-preserved facade is decorated with a rich variety of symbols related to death: Nabatean gods in charge of guiding the souls of the dead, Medusa heads, eagles and winged victories.

THE OUTER SIQ

An opening in the brilliant red and pink stone mountainside to the right of the Treasury leads to the theatre and the city centre. As if to make sure that visitors have no mistake about the importance the Nabateans of Petra placed on

Left: *First glimpse of the Treasury as seen upon emerging from the Siq*
Below: *The awe-inspiring Treasury*

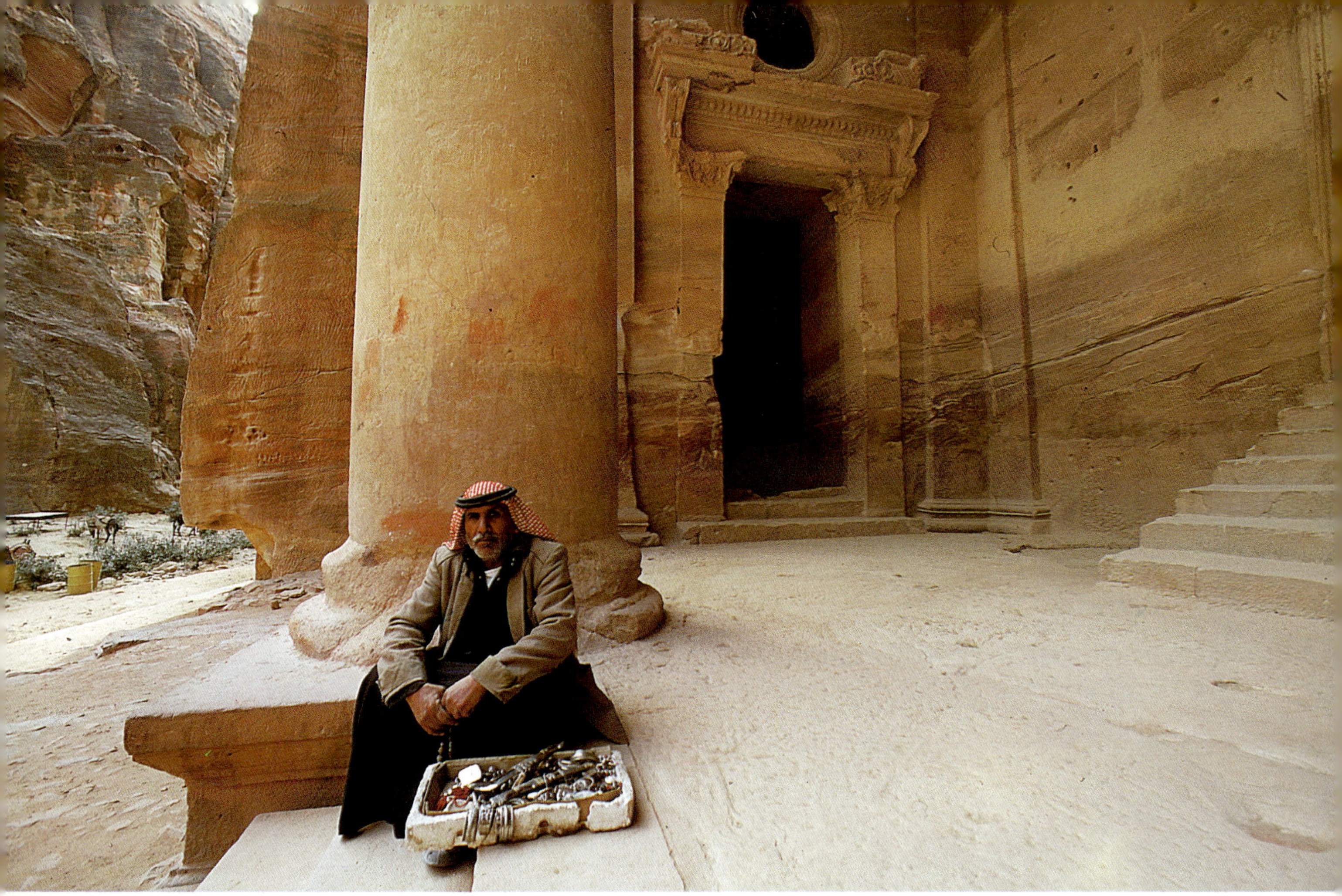
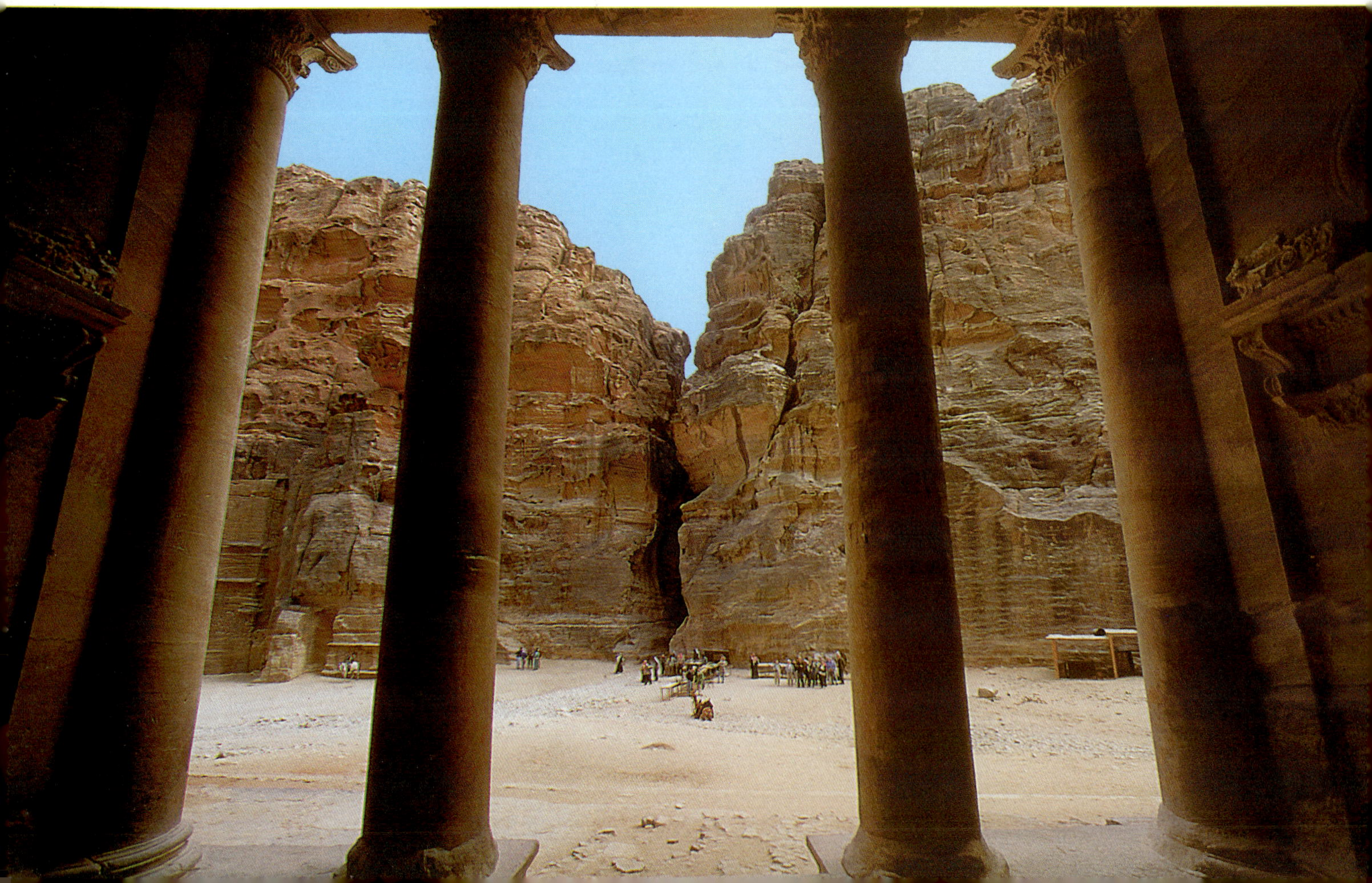

honouring their dead, the passageway - called the Outer Siq-is lined with countless tombs cut into the stone mountains.

At the base of the cliffs that make up the Outer Siq, Beduin boys and men sell a variety of souvenirs, including Nabatean coins and other relics, as well as imitations. The best-known souvenirs of Petra, however, are bottles of coloured sand depicting camels, mountains and other scenes from the Rose-Red City. The tradition of arranging different colours of sand in bottles has been around for the past few decades - making it a very new craft, by Nabatean standards!

THE THEATRE

It may look Roman, but this theatre was built by the Nabateans between 4 BC and 27 AD in the same painstaking fashion that they built all of Petra. All 33 rows of seats, with enough space to seat 7,000, were carved into a stone mountainside. Considering the tools available to them and the level of exactitude with which they completed their work, the theatre is far more impressive than any typical Roman counterpart.

Far Left: *Outside the Treasury*
Left: *Nabatean facade*
Below Left: *View of the Siq from within the Treasury*
Below: *The Nabateans' theatre, set in the middle of their holy burial ground, has 33 rows of seats carved into the stone*

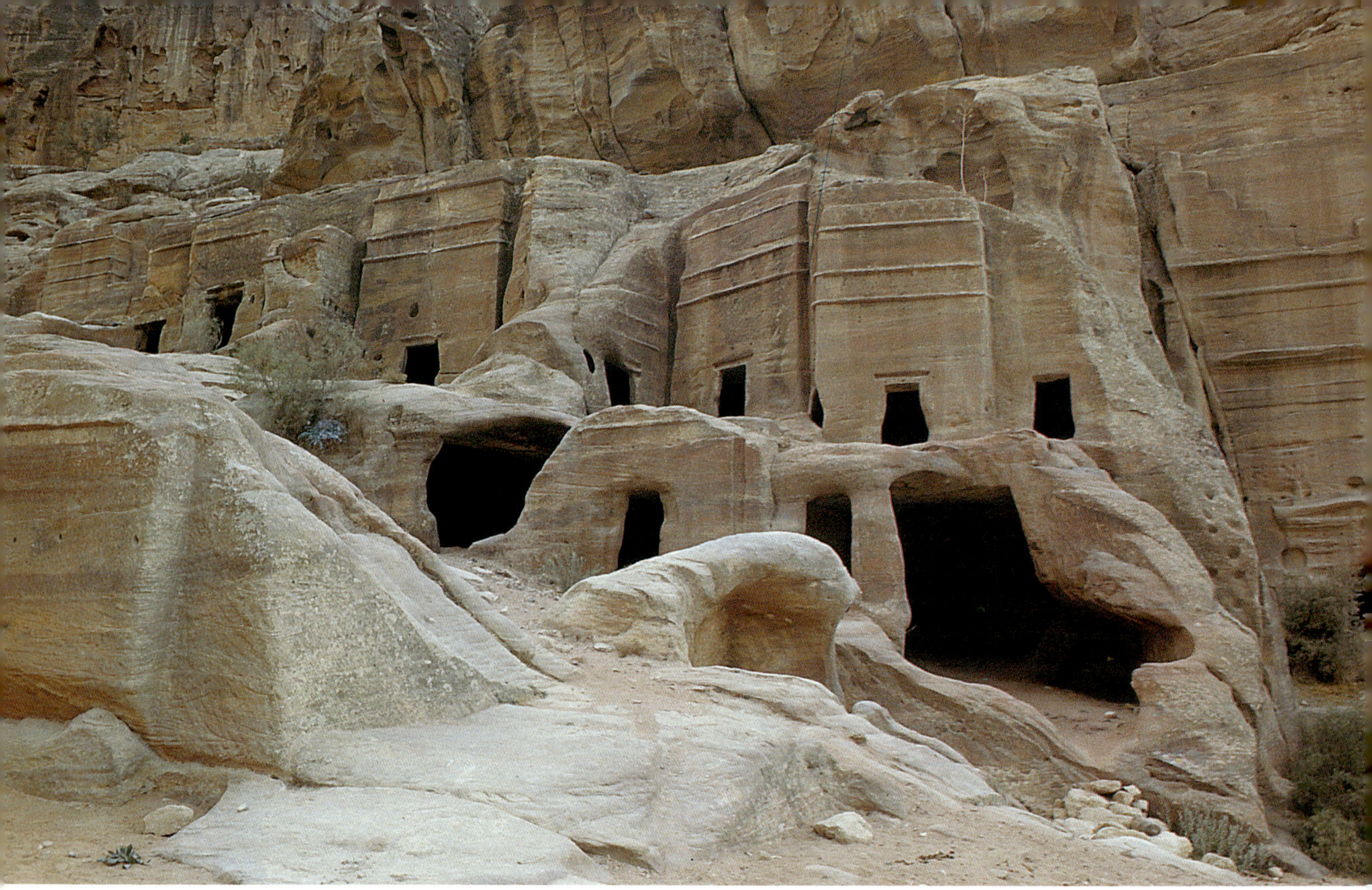

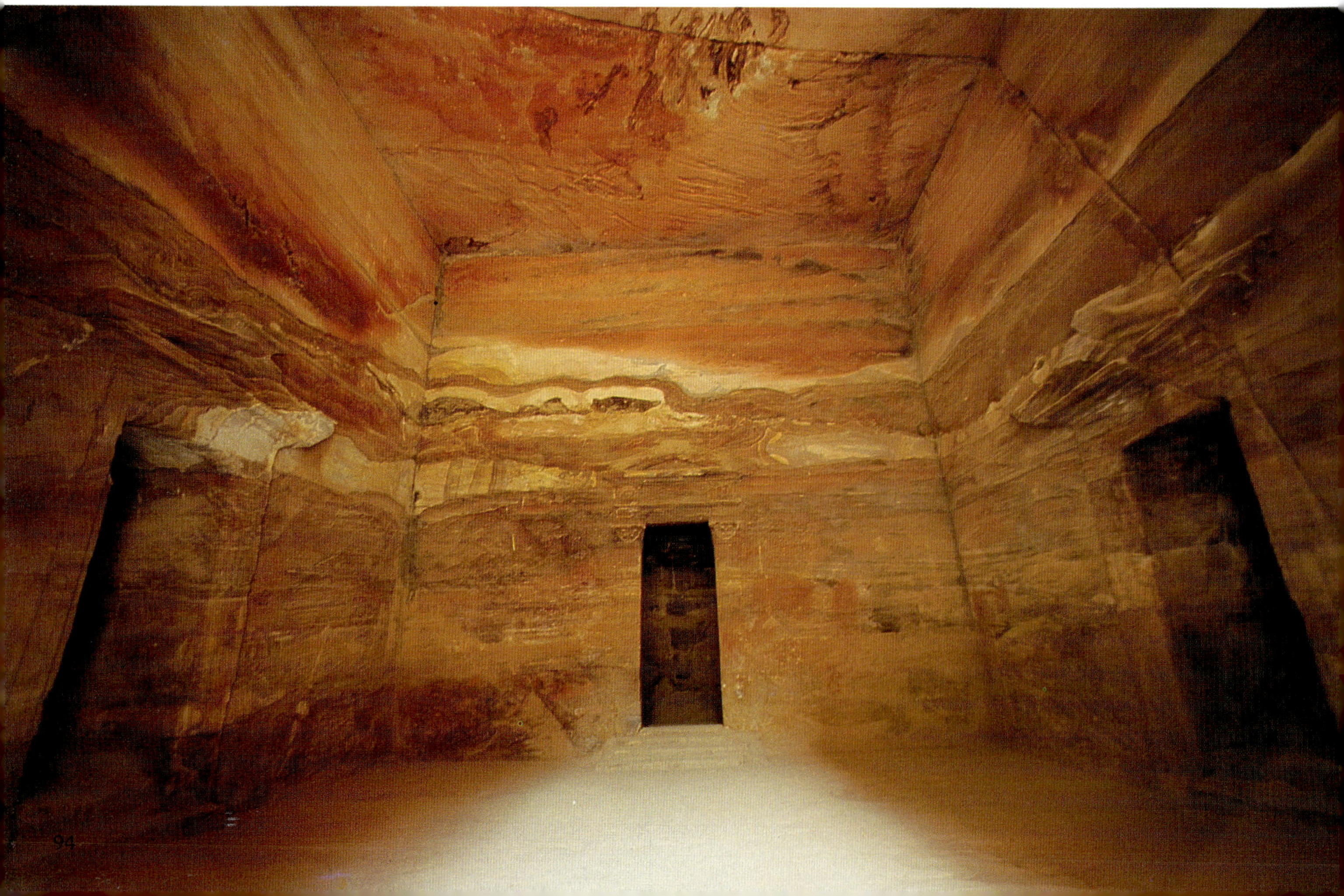

Above: The altar at the High Place of Sacrifice
Left: A symbol of a Nabatean god - or a roadside marker?
Overleaf Page 96:
Top Left: Roman Soldier Tomb
Top Right: Renaissance Tomb
Bottom: Interior of the Triclinium

Scholarly opinion is divided as to whether the theatre was used for entertainment and political gatherings - like many other theatres in the region - or for gatherings of a religious nature. Given the setting in the midst of a giant cemetery, far from the city centre, this latter suggestion may be realistic.

Locating the theatre in a central place along the Street of Facades must have been of great importance to the Nabateans, for they destroyed and damaged many burial rooms in order to carve the rows of seats into the stone.

THE HIGH PLACE OF SACRIFICE

Set on a hilltop some 200 metres above the royal tombs and outer siq, the High Place of Sacrifice offers a more challenging destination to hikers, and a glimpse of many more Nabatean wonders along the way.

The three-hour roundtrip hike usually begins with a sharp ascent behind the theatre. As you reach the High Place,

you'll see two obelisks, which may be the Nabateans' images of their two most important gods. The High Place of Sacrifice itself consists of a large platform that has been cut onto the mountaintop. Surrounded by benches carved into the stone, there are two altars for sacrifice. Each comes, equipped with a small cistern for water used for ritual purposes, and a drainage system to carry away the blood of the sacrificed animals (scholars believe the Nabateans in Petra made only animal - not human - sacrifices.)

Page 97:
Top Left: *Zibb Pharoun*
Top Right: *Lion Monument*
Bottom: *Wadi Farasa*
Right: *Qasr el-Bint*
Below: *The Arched Gate*
Left Below: *Beduin woman selling souvenirs*
Opposite Page: *The Colonnaded Street - Petra's main avenue - with a view of the Royal Tombs*

THE ROYAL TOMBS

Many details about the Royal Tombs, opposite the theatre, remain unclear. Scholars agree that they are, indeed, tombs, but the only reason they are deemed to be royal is that they are so elaborate.

At the top of the stairs to the tombs, the Urn Tomb is the first to be encountered. The name stems from a small urn perched on the facade's upper pediment. The local Beduin have other names for the tomb, including the Court and the Jail. In 446, the Byzantines converted the inner hall into a church.

North of the Urn Tomb, separated by several other facades, is the Corinthian Tomb, which incorporates a small-scale copy of the Treasury in its facade. Next door is the Palace Tomb. Originally three storeys high, the massive facade's third storey was built atop the rock. As if to bear testament to Nabatean construction, the third storey has all but collapsed over the ages. The first two storeys, chiseled into the mountain, survive for all to see.

Opposite Page and Below: *Archeological finds in Petra*
Opposite Above: *The grounds of the archeology museum*

TEMPLE OF THE WINGED LIONS

Built around 27 AD, the temple was dedicated to one of the Nabateans' female gods. This was a central point of life in Petra until a fire destroyed much of the structure in the early second century. After that, it served as dwellings for Nabatean families, until the 363 earthquake levelled it. Finds from the archeological excavations here are on display in the archeological museum in Petra.

THE LION MONUMENT

There used to be many routes to the High Place of Sacrifice, but only two remain accessible today. After completing your visit atop the High Place, head down via Wadi Farasa. Just before a steep staircase, you will pass the Lion Monument, a huge chiseled rendering of a lion. Measuring five metres in length, the lion serves as a ritual fountain along the route to the High Place. Water from the High Place passed through the lion's mouth before flowing down to the city centre.

ROMAN SOLDIER TOMB AND TRICLINIUM

After passing dozens more wall tombs, you will reach the Roman Soldier Tomb and Triclinium. In the past, these two places were linked by a central colonnaded courtyard. The Roman Soldier Tomb's facade is adorned by three

figures in Roman military dress, indicating that the site was either built or remodelled after the Romans annexed Petra in 106 AD. The Triclinium is strikingly different from most of the structures surviving in Petra, Its facade is simple, while its interior is the most ornate found in the city. It was the funerary banquet hall for the Roman Soldier Tomb, and may have been part of a larger complex.

Right: *Nabatean tombs*
Below: *The Red Rock of Petra comes in many shades*
Bottom Left: *Lion's Tomb*
Bottom Right: *Wadi Siyyagh*
Opposite Page: *The Royal Tombs; on the left is the Palace Tomb; and on the right is the Corinthian Tomb*

102

ED-DEIR (THE MONASTERY)

The hike through Wadi ed-Deir is a pleasant - if uphill - trek that passes several impressive Nabatean monuments. The advantage of being in a continual ascent is that the trail offers striking views of the entire central part of Petra.

Upon reaching the clearing at the end of the trail, you will turn to face ed-Deir, the largest edifice in all of Petra. Measuring 45 metres by 50 metres, the facade was completed in the mid-first century AD and it served as a feasting hall in honour of the dead.

By the time visitors reach ed-Deir, the design and style seem familiar. The facade is a larger, less-ornate version of that found at the Treasury. Like the Treasury, this edifice's name also has no bearing on its function. It has been called the Monastery in English because at the back of the hall there are several crosses carved and painted on the walls. This is probably a reflection of the Christian use of the place in the fourth or fifth centuries.

Opposite Page:
Top: *Ed-Deir (the Monastery)*
Bottom Left: *Blue lizards are common in Petra*
Bottom Right: *Siq al-Barid*

Right: *Entry to Siq al-Barid*
Below: *Facade of what may have been a home or a temple in Siq al-Barid*

WU'EIRA

This is another castle built by King Baldwin I of Jerusalem. Located just north of Petra, it was protected on three sides by steep cliffs, and on the fourth side by an even steeper descent into Wadi Shab Qeis below. Access today is via a narrow bridge.

Baldwin I built this castle in 1115-1116, and it remained in Crusader hands until all of the Crusader castles in Jordan capitulated to Saleh a-Din in 1189, following his conquest of Jerusalem.

SIQ AL-BARID (LITTLE PETRA)

Built in the first century AD, this was a well-to-do suburb of the Nabatean capital city, Petra. The trade routes which extended north and west passed through Little Petra, and the area served as the main commercial and farming centre for the Petra area. Huge cisterns built into the stone stored the water needed for residential and agricultural use. Indeed, the local Beduin still use the cisterns.

Unlike in Petra itself, where the chiseled facades all were associated with death, some of the facades cut into the red mountains of Siq al-Barid seem clearly to have been used as dwellings for the living.

AL-BEIDHA

This remarkable Neolithic village offers some of the best-preserved remains from the period of 7000-6500 BC in the entire Middle East. Where else do so many other details of such an ancient village remain in such good condition today?

Al-Beidha offers a remarkable glimpse of life in the period when man was making the transition from hunting and gathering to a settled life in year-round homes. The people's experimentation with the new idea of living in a permanent home is here for all to see: the houses are in a variety of shapes, including squares and circles. Even much of the plaster remains in good condition.

JABAL HAROUN (MT. AARON)

More than 1,300 metres above sea level, this peak is the highest point in the area. It commands a panoramic view of the entire Red Rock City, the surrounding desert and beyond.

Getting here is a difficult challenge which should not be undertaken without an accompanying Beduin guide. The shrine, where Moses' brother Aaron is believed to have died and been buried, is particularly holy to the local population, so any visit must be made with appropriate reverence. Scholars are unsure that this is the site of Mt. Hor, which the Bible identifies as Aaron's burial place. But the locals don't need any scholars' certainty. They believe.

WADI RUM

The towering mountains and natural rock formations of Wadi Rum mesmerized Lawrence of Arabia and many others who preceded and followed him. A bit off the

Opposite Page: *Aerial view of Wadi Rum*
Below: *Seven Pillars*
Bottom: *The Beduin guard Wadi Rum to this day*
Right: *Encountering Wadi Rùm's natural beauty*

Previous Pages, This Page and Overleaf: *Scenes on the trails of Wadi Rum*

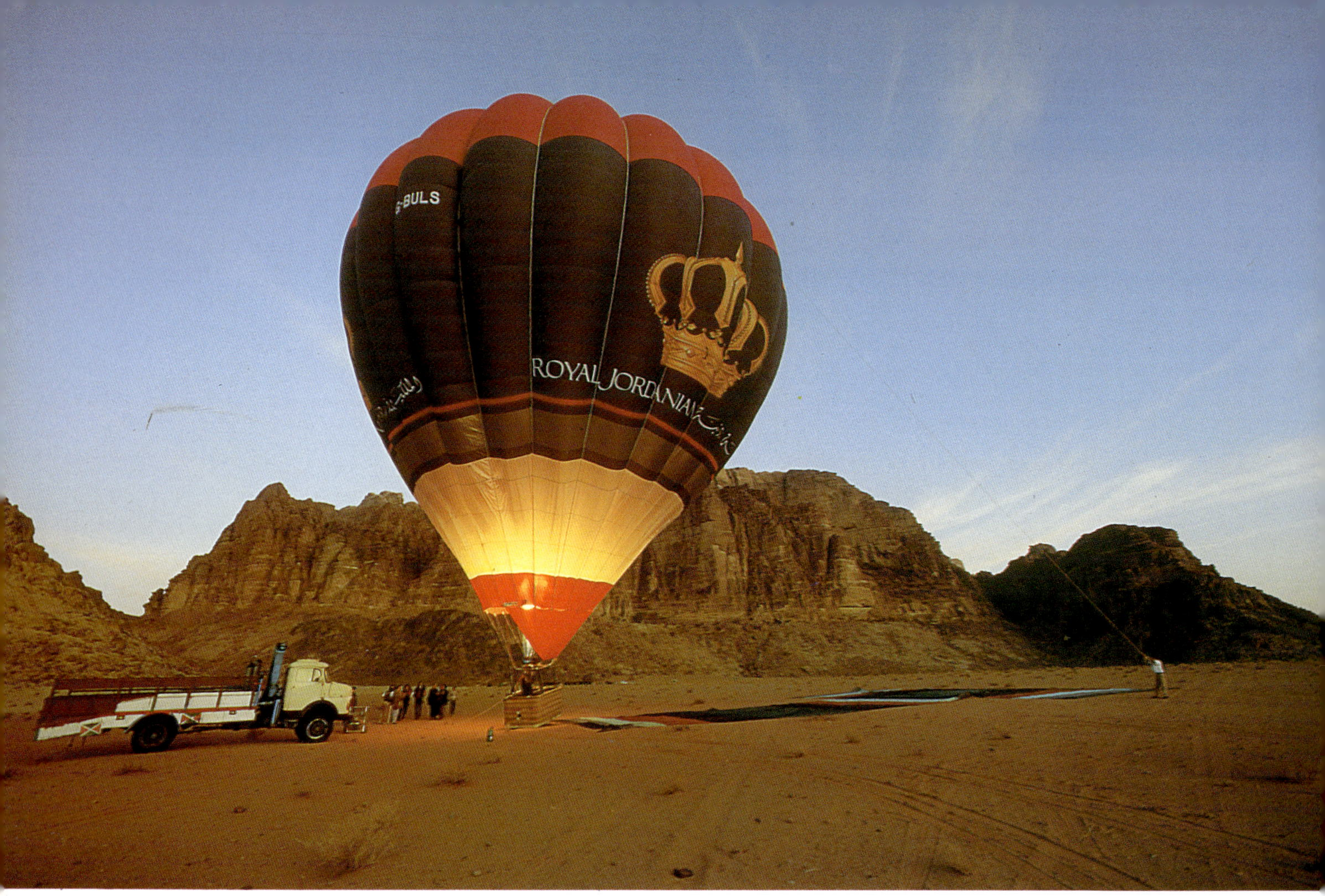
G-BULS
ROYAL JORDANIAN

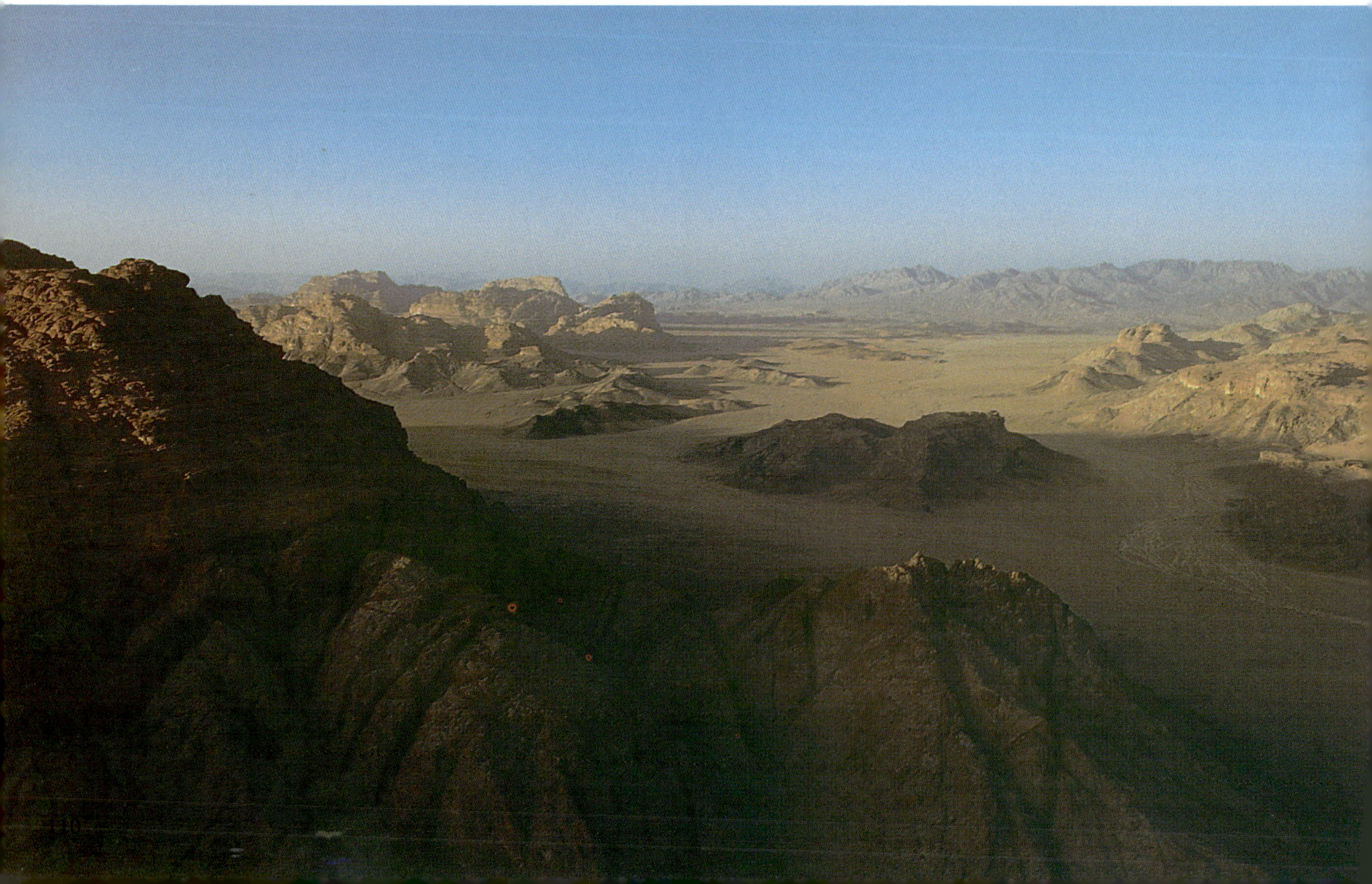

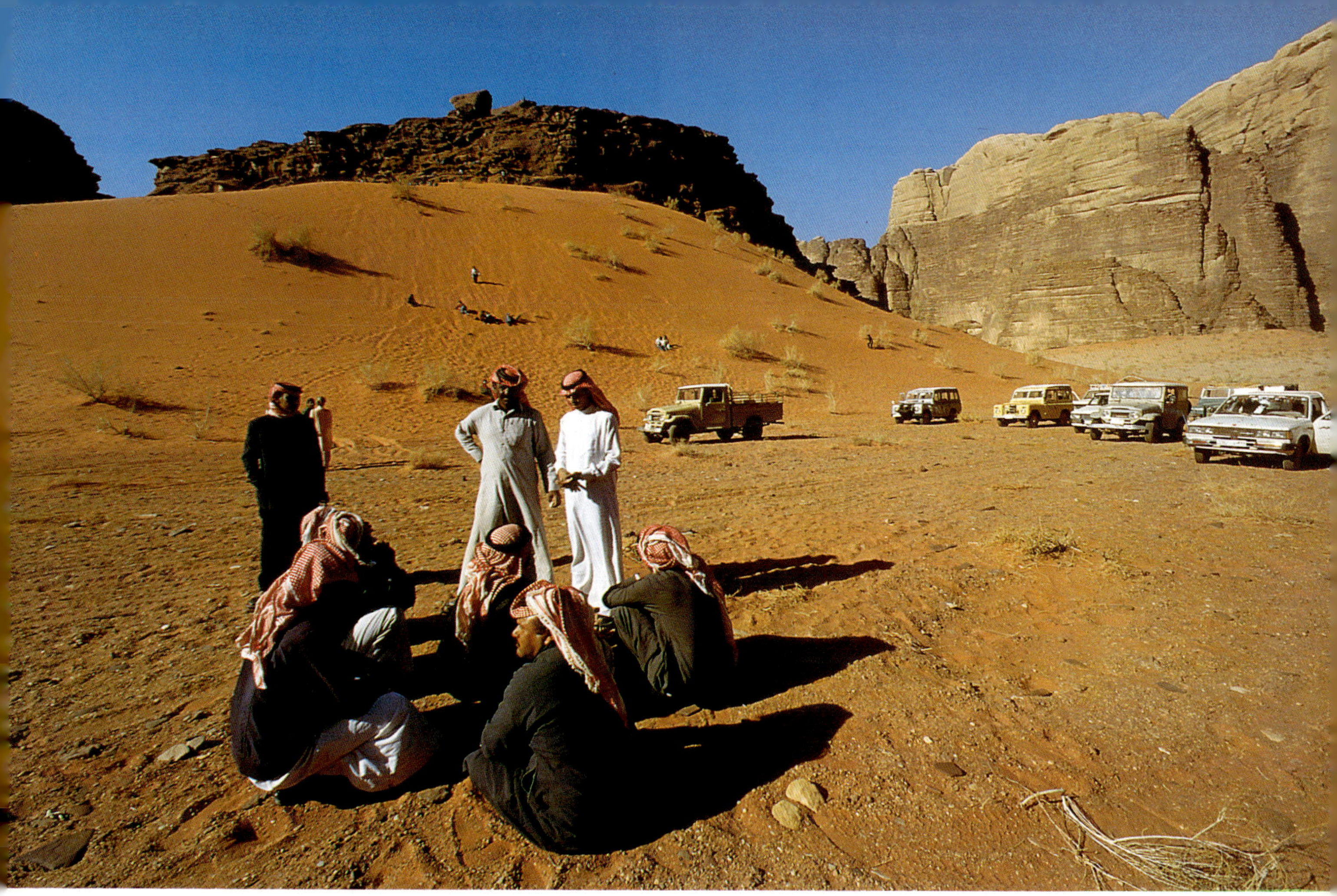

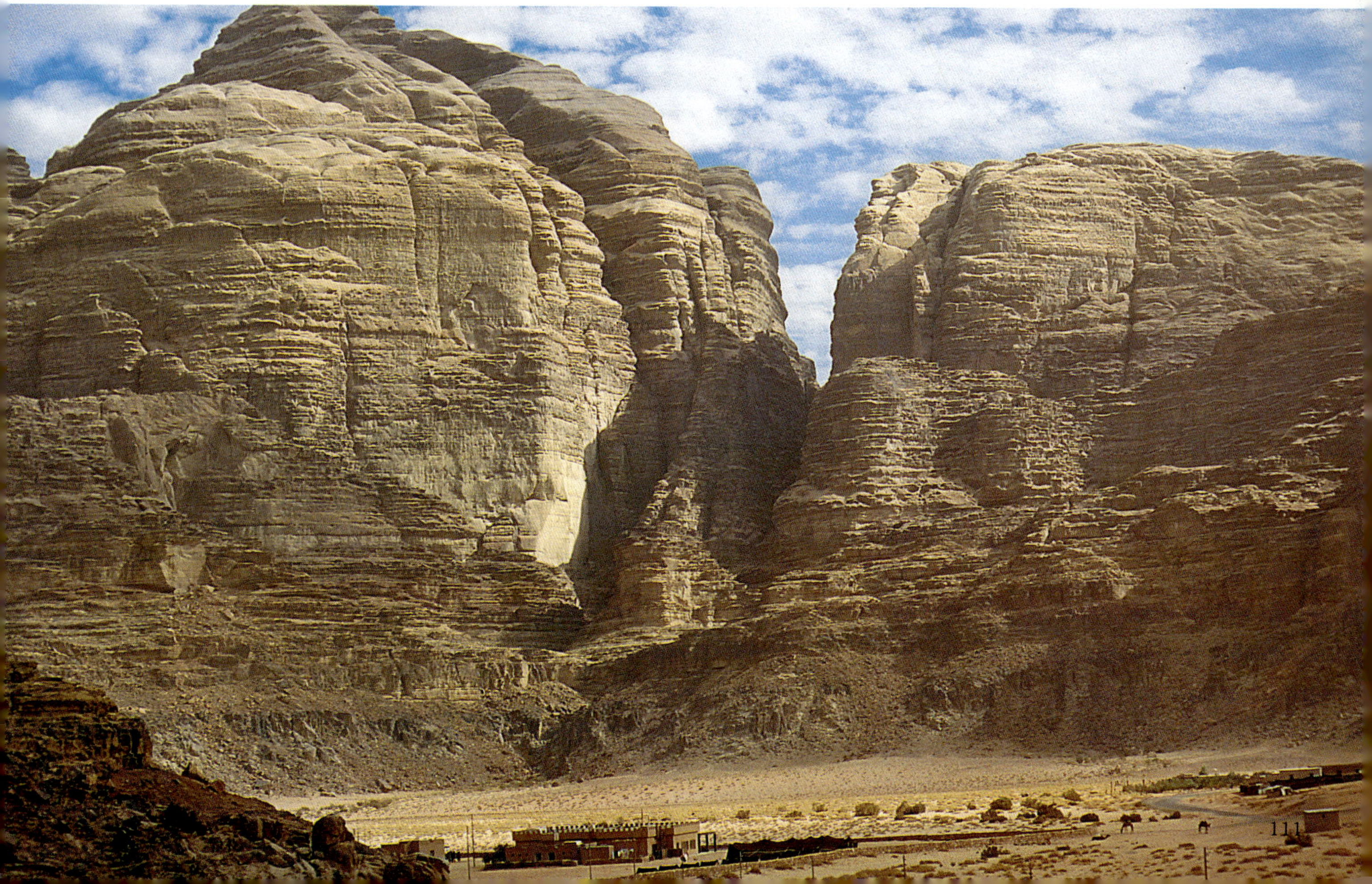

beaten track, due east of Aqaba, the striking natural beauty has not been destroyed by an overload of tourists. In The *Seven Pillars of Wisdom*, T.E. Lawrence wrote eloquently about the region he had come to love so dearly: " The sun had sunk behind the western wall, leaving the pit in shadow, but its dying glare flooded with startling red the wings each side of the entry, and the fiery bulk of the further wall across the great valley. The pit floor was of damp sand, darkly wooded with shrubs, while about the feet of all the cliffs lay boulders greater than houses, sometimes indeed like fortresses which had crashed down from the heights above. In front of us a path, pale with use, zigzagged up the cliff to the point from which the main face rose, and there it turned precariously southward along a shallow ledge outlined by occasional leafy trees. From between these trees, in hidden crannies of the rock, issued strange cries; the echoes, turned into music, of the voices of the Arabs watering camels at the spring which there flowed out 300 feet above ground."

Lawrence's unbridled enthusiasm practically leaps off the page and tells readers that if they visit Wadi Rum, they will be amply rewarded. Indeed, perhaps the only sight as

Left and below: *Nabatean temple*
Following Pages: *Nature takes your breath away*

beautiful as the sunrise at Wadi Rum is the sunset. The sheer cliffs and the gaping spaces between mountain ridges all add up to create scenes that cannot be imagined without being seen.

TRACES OF ANCIENT LIFE

The ruins of a great Nabatean temple at the foot of Jebel Rum is just one indication that this area was an important part of the Nabatean empire, which was based further north, in Petra. Byzantine ruins can also be found.

More recent signs of life come in the form of odd-looking graffiti that appear on countless large boulders along the track leading through the area. Similar inscriptions are found along old trade routes as far south as Saudi Arabia, and as far north as Ma'an. They have been left over the centuries by generations of traders who passed along these routes on their camels.

The Thamud tribe, which controlled the route from its base in Saudi Arabia over the centuries, used a South Semitic alphabet which has little in common with Nabatean or Arabic, which are based on North Semitic script.

More recently, Glubb Pasha built a fort here in 1933 for the Desert Police force he had established. Today, the Beduin officers - who still wear the sharp garb that Glubb Pasha himself designed more than 60 years ago - patroling in Wadi Rum are as much a tourist sensation as anything else.

116

AQABA

The Red Sea port city of Aqaba plays an important role in Jordan's economic life, and its holiday resources are practically limitless. The shoreline boasts sandy beaches, and the blue-green water is home to brilliant coral reefs and a wide variety of fish.

Fish are an attraction on shore as well as off. Aqaba is Jordan's fastest-growing city today, and its growing selection of restaurants offers fried and grilled fish dishes alongside traditional Middle Eastern grilled meats and salads.

Aqaba is more than a modern Jordanian success story. It is also an ancient city with a rich history. Furnaces have been unearthed which were used for smelting the copper mined in Wadi Araba as far back as 3500 BC. Later, King Solomon built and maintained a fleet of ships to export copper.

Over the centuries, Aqaba has also been controlled by the Edomites, the Nabateans, the Ptolemies, the Romans, the Byzantines, the Arabs, the Crusaders, the Ottomans and, finally, the Hashemites.

Its name has changed almost as many times as its sovereignty. The Bible calls the settlements here Elath, Eloth and Ezion-Geber. The Ptolemies called it Berenice, while the Romans named it Ailana.

The Arabs changed the name to Ayla. Finally, in the thirteenth century, it came to be called Aqaba, and the name has stuck for more than seven centuries.

Above: *Wadi Rum*
Right: *Sunning in Aqaba*

MEDIEVAL FORTRESS

South of the city, near the waterfront, stands a medieval fortress whose exact origins are something of a mystery. While presumably the Crusaders built it, all of the markings inside speak of construction by the Arabs between the fourteenth and sixteenth centuries. The Arabs used it primarily as a fortified rest stop for Egyptian pilgrims en route to or from Mecca.

Lawrence of Arabia played a key role in winning back Aqaba for the Arabs in 1917, and it has been in Hashemite hands ever since.

Below: Panoramic city view
Right: Excavations at Ayla
Opposite Page: Street scenes around Aqaba

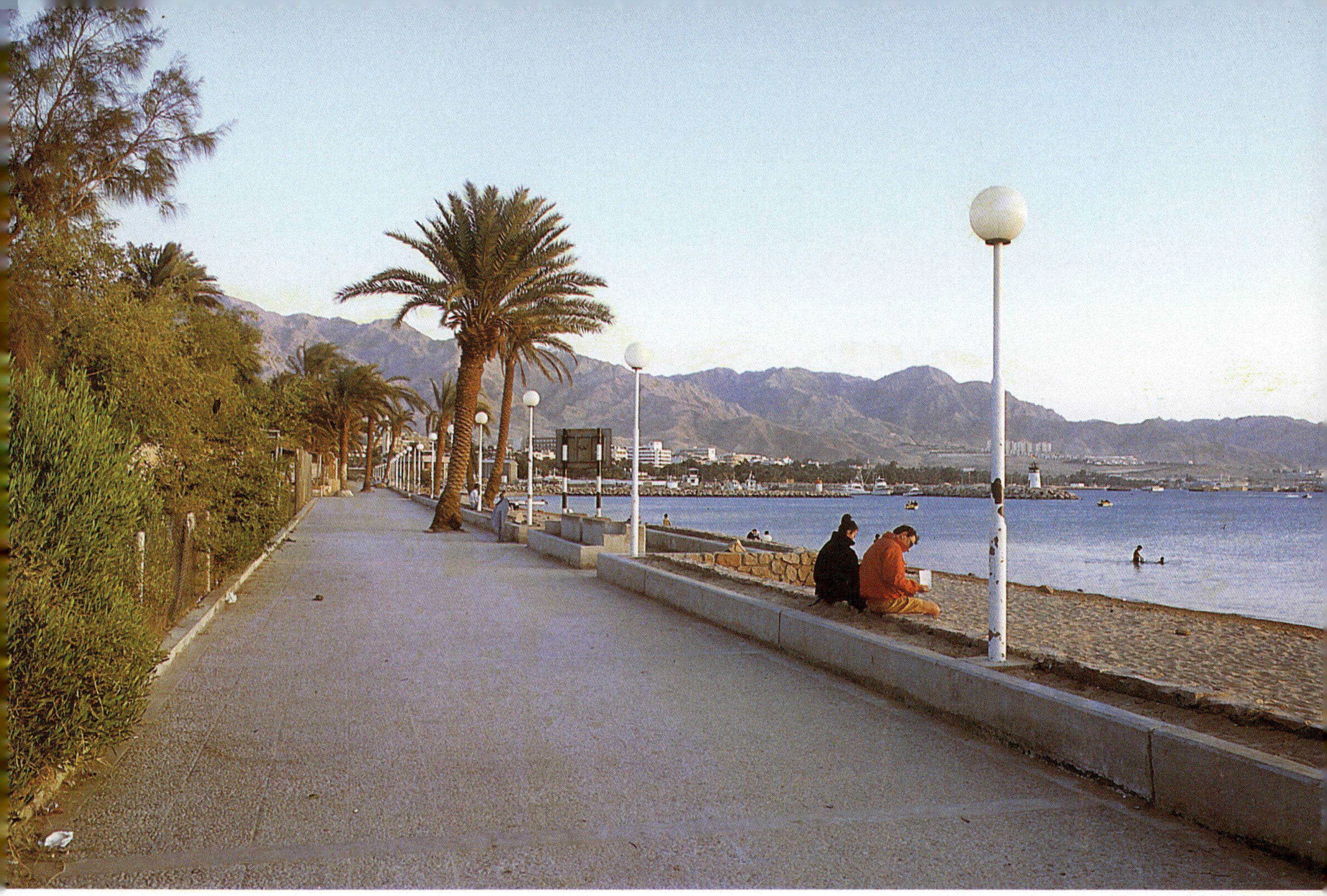

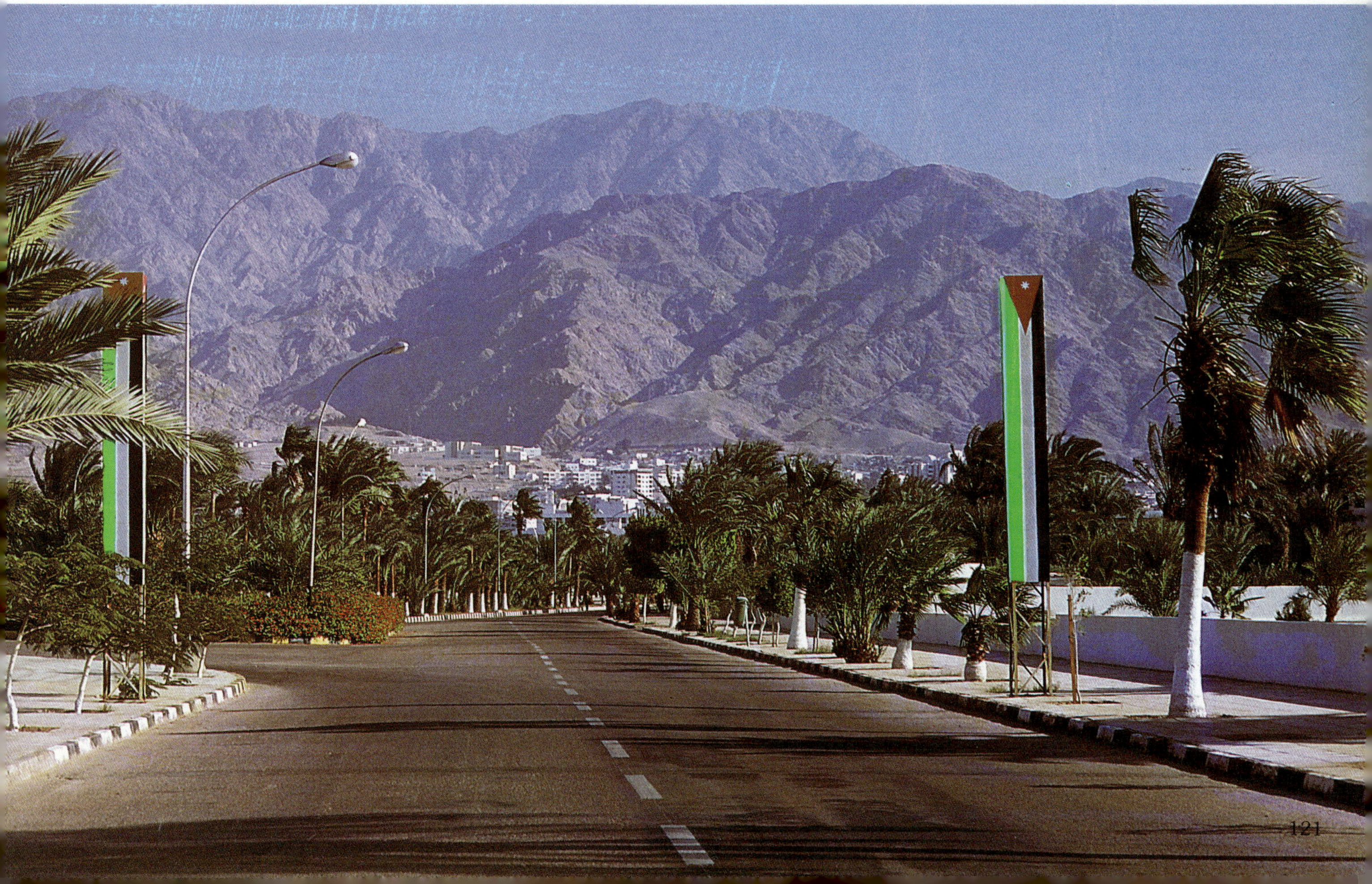

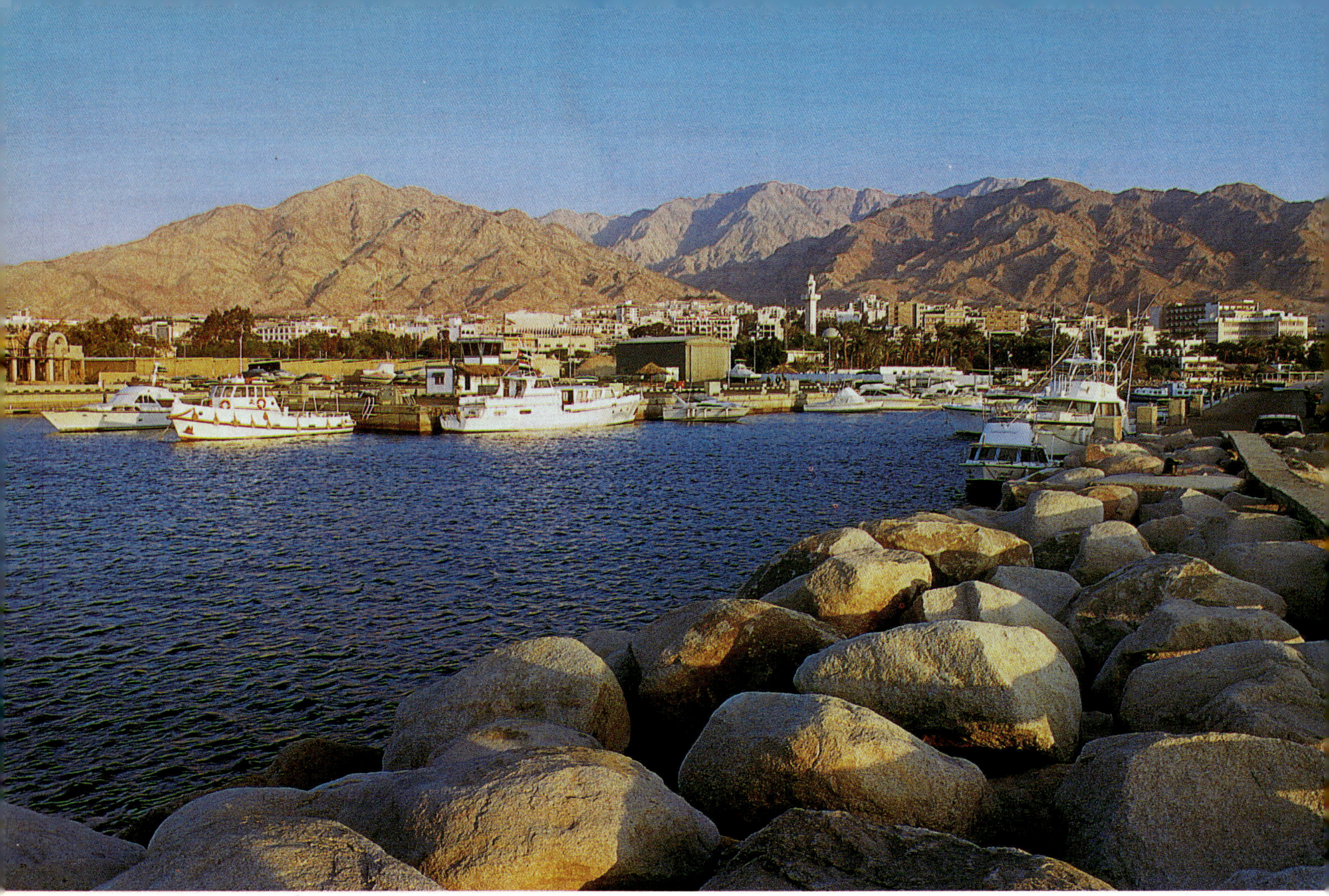

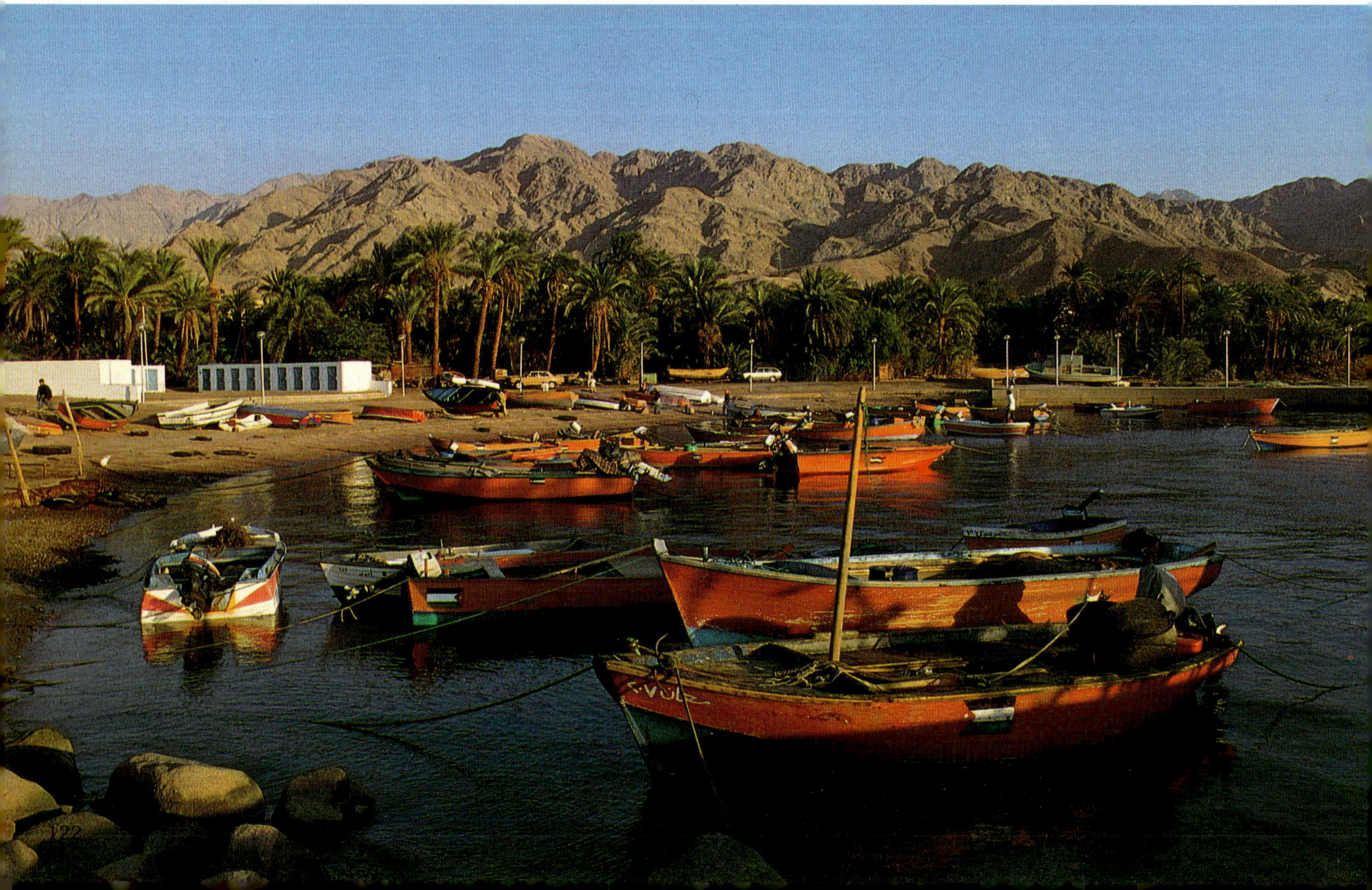

Opposite Page:
Top and Bottom: *Aqaba's marina is filled with vessels that run the gamut from simple rowboats to luxury cruisers.*

Above: *Royal Jordanian Riding Club*
Below: *Unspoiled Red Sea shores*

Overleaf Page 124:
Top: *Vegetable market in Aqaba*
Bottom: *Typical souvenir shop*
Page 125: *Aqaba offers all kinds of water sports*

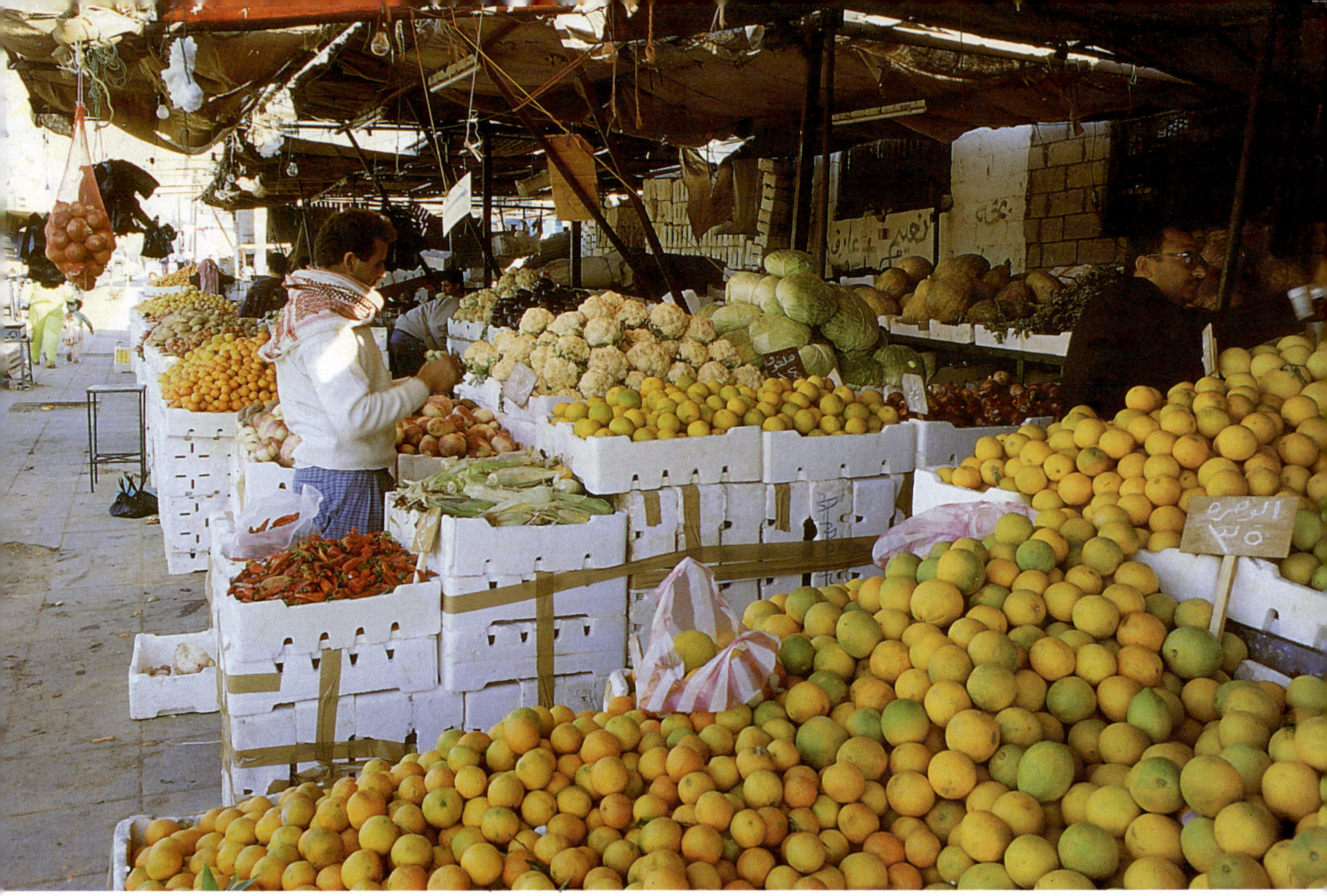

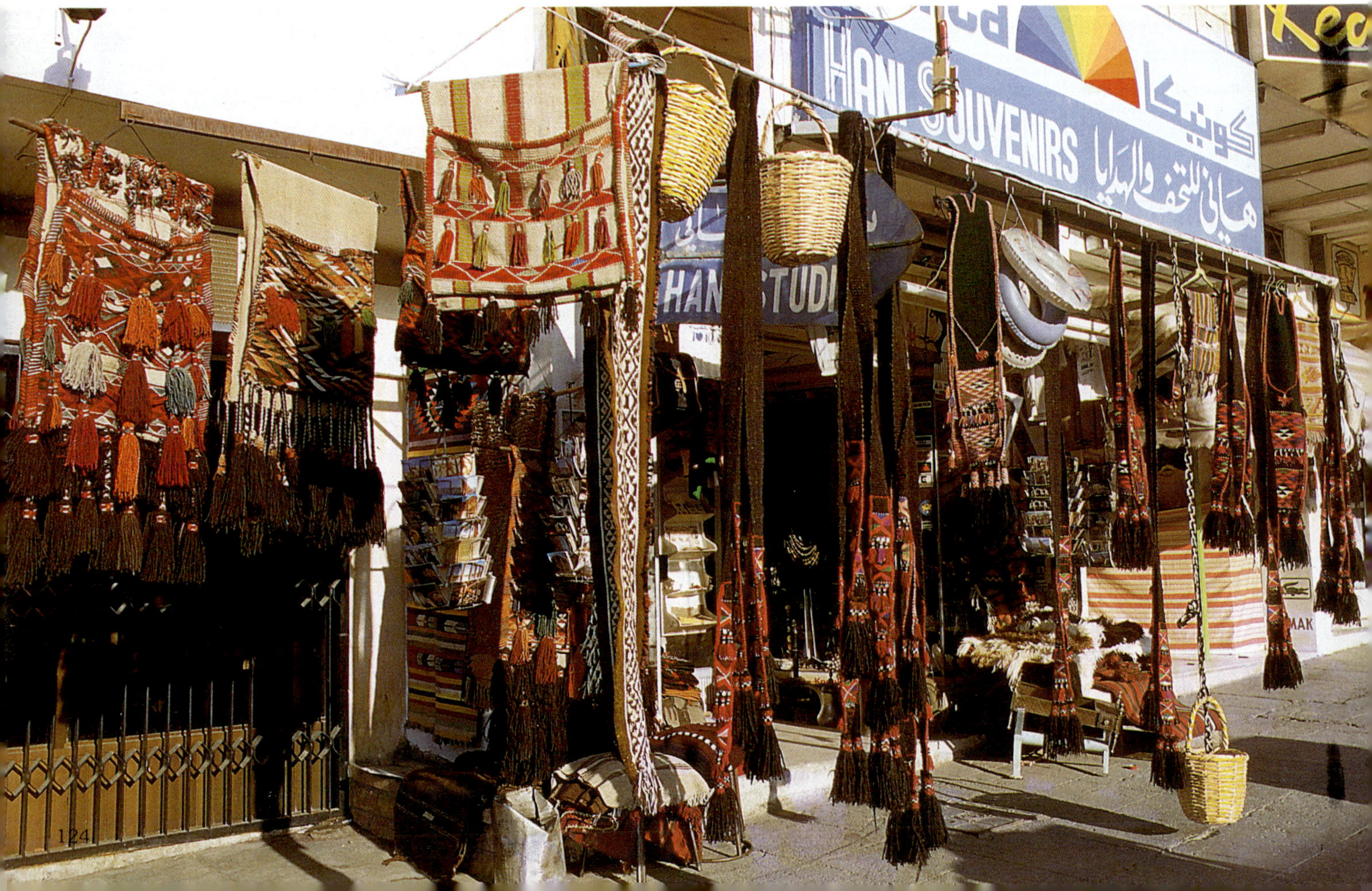
HANI SOUVENIRS
هاني للتحف والهدايا

Overleaf: Underwater coral reefs and fish boggle the mind with their bursts of brilliant colour

Page 127:

Top: City view

Bottom: Medieval fort

UNDERWATER ATTRACTIONS

Aqaba's underwater delights are among the world's best. The less-frequented beaches along the approach to the Saudi Arabian border offer a wild array of coral reefs and fish. With just a snorkel and a pair of fins, anyone can become a great underwater explorer. And trained scuba divers who go deeper see much, much more.

If you want to see the marine life without getting wet, take a ride on a glass-bottomed boat or visit the Marine Research Centre's aquarium.

Aqaba's hotel and beachfront tourism services offer a full range of water sports, including water skiing, parasailing and boating. The eager-to-learn can take accredited scuba diving courses that culminate in receipt of an international diver's certificate.

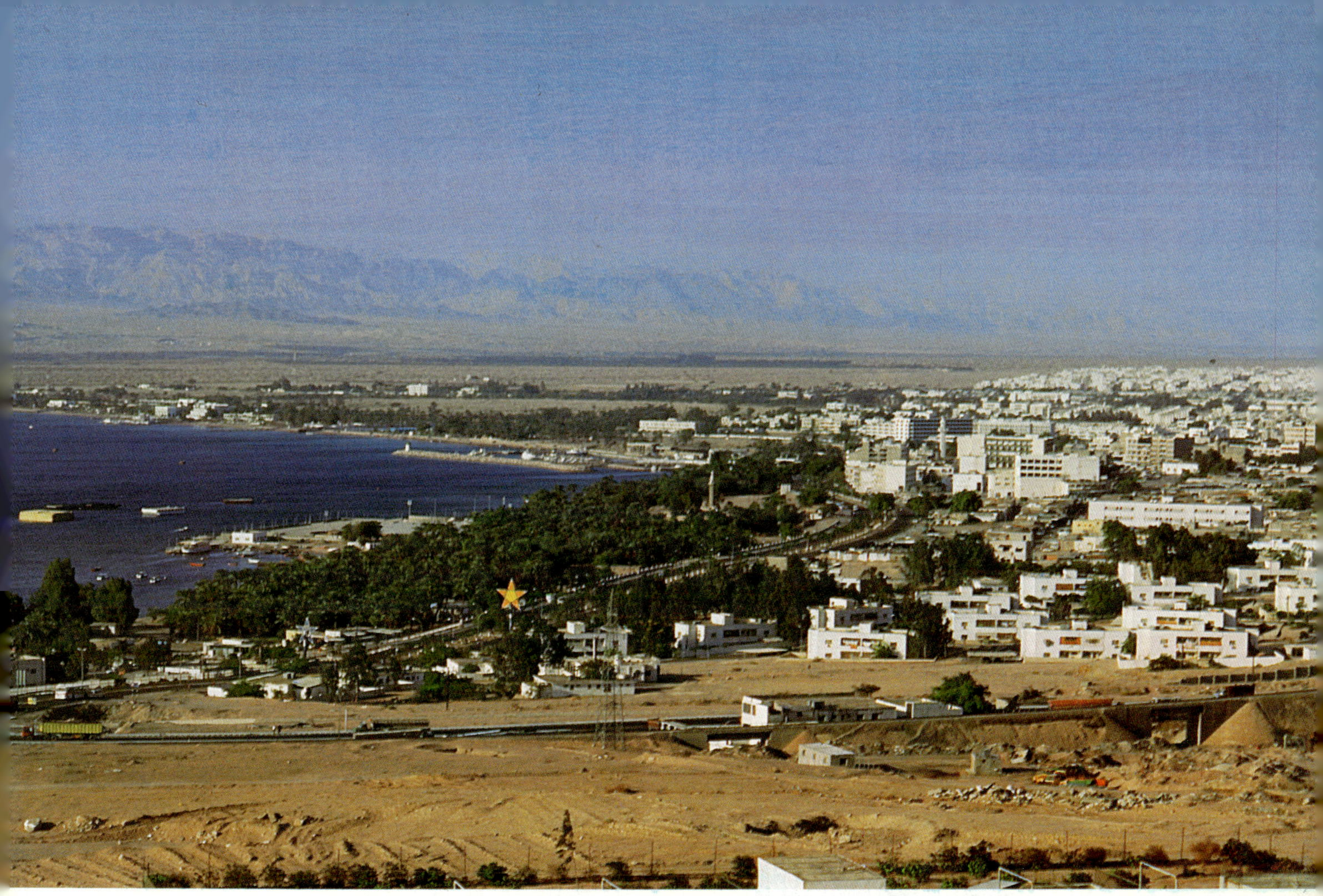

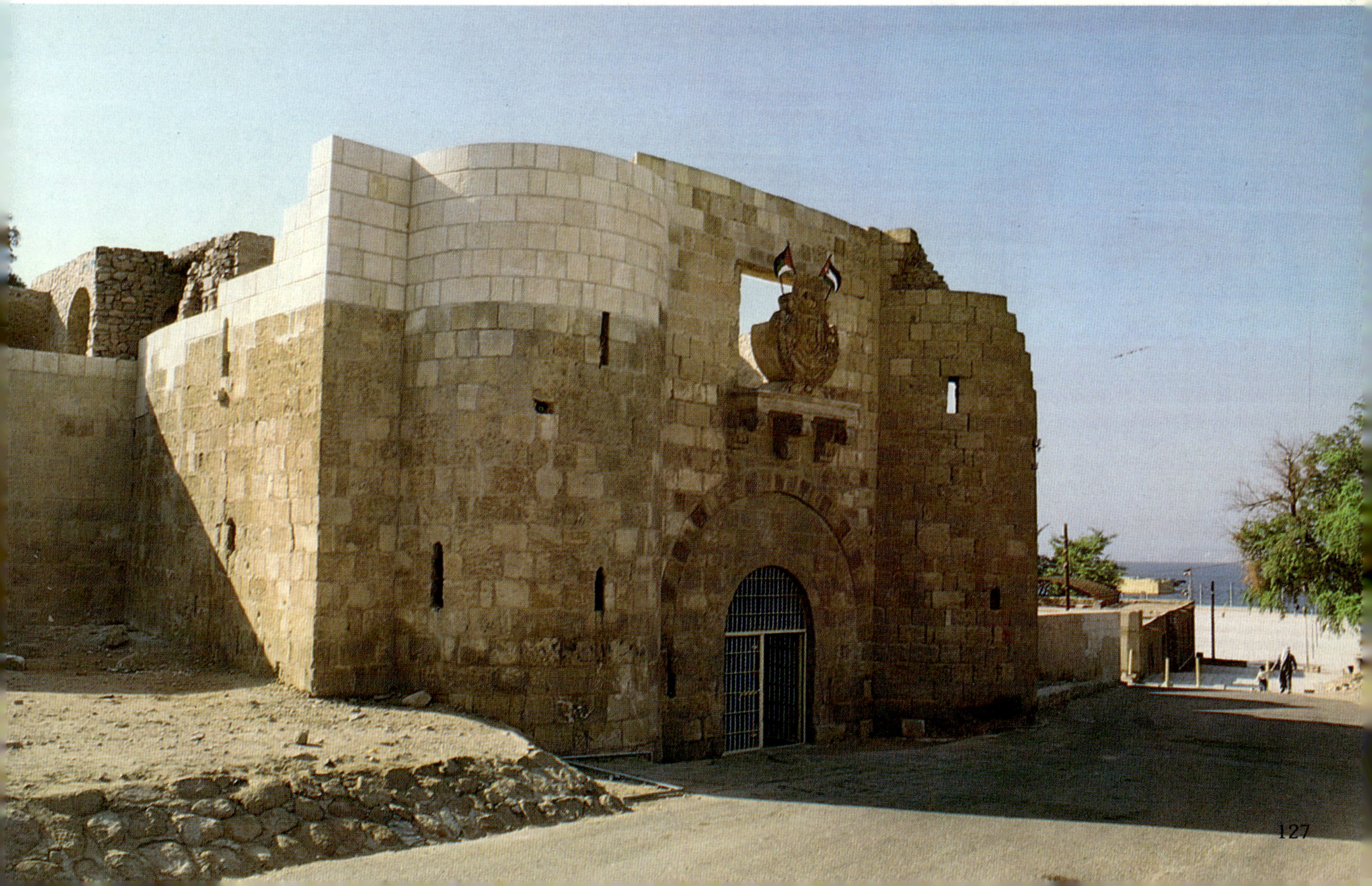